THE BUSY SCRAPPER

Making the mos
your scrapbooking

MEMORY
MAKERS
BOOKS

Cincinnati, Ohio

www.mycraftivity.com

12 11 10 09 08   5 4 3 2 1

Distributed in Canada by Fraser Direct
100 Armstrong Avenue
Georgetown, ON, Canada L7G 5S4
Tel: (905) 877-4411

Distributed in the U.K. and Europe by David & Charles
Brunel House, Newton Abbot, Devon, TQ12 4PU, England
Tel: (+44) 1626 323200, Fax: (+44) 1626 323319
E-mail: postmaster@davidandcharles.co.uk

Distributed in Australia by Capricorn Link
P.O. Box 704, S. Windsor, NSW 2756 Australia
Tel: (02) 4577-3555

Library of Congress Cataloging-in-Publication Data

Walsh, Courtney
   The busy scrapper : making the most of your scrapbooking
time / Courtney Walsh. — 1st ed.
      p. cm.
   Includes index.
   ISBN 978-1-59963-029-8 (pbk. : alk. paper)
 1. Photograph albums. 2. Photographs—Conservation and
restoration. 3. Scrapbooking. I. Memory Makers Books (Firm)
II. Title.
   TR501.W346 2008
   745.593—dc22
                                        2008022966

Editor: Kristin Boys
Designer: Kelly O'Dell
Art Coordinator: Eileen Aber
Production Coordinator: Greg Nock
Photographer: Al Parrish
Illustrator: Lisa Ballard, Scott Hull Associates

fw
F+W PUBLICATIONS, INC.
www.publications.com

About the Author
Courtney Walsh

Whether she's writing, scrapbooking or lugging a goggle-wearing four-year-old around Wal-Mart, Courtney Walsh is passionate about making checkmarks on her to-do list! Busy in the best sense of the word, Courtney is the mother of three children and wife to an equally busy children's pastor. She is also the author of *Scrapbooking Your Faith* and a former contributing editor to *Memory Makers* magazine. With a very full life, she set out to discover some doable ways to fit scrapbooking into the daily grind. This book is the result of that research.

Metric Conversion Chart

to convert	to	multiply by
Inches	Centimeters	2.54
Centimeters	Inches	0.4
Feet	Centimeters	30.5
Centimeters	Feet	0.03
Yards	Meters	0.9
Meters	Yards	1.1
Sq. Inches	Sq. Centimeters	6.45
Sq. Centimeters	Sq. Inches	0.16
Sq. Feet	Sq. Meters	0.09
Sq. Meters	Sq. Feet	10.8
Sq. Yards	Sq. Meters	0.8
Sq. Meters	Sq. Yards	1.2
Pounds	Kilograms	0.45
Kilograms	Pounds	2.2
Ounces	Grams	28.3
Grams	Ounces	0.035

Dedication

I would be remiss if I didn't dedicate this book to the three people who make my life the busiest (and, in addition to my husband, the best!)

→ Sophia
→ Ethan
→ & Sam

I never thought I would love being a mommy so much, but you three are what keep me going. You make me the happiest (and sometimes the craziest), and I am so blessed to get to hang out with you all day long. Thank you for making my life the whirlwind that it is ... otherwise I might not have seen the need for this book in the first place! Here's to you!

Acknowledgments

To the greatest husband ever! Adam, I absolutely love my life with you, and your support of my writing just makes me want to go for it more! Thank you for changing diapers, doing laundry and handling household crises whenever I needed some "work time." We make an awfully great team!

To my extended family, whose faces appear on my scrapbook pages on a pretty regular basis: my mom and dad, my brother, Chad, and sister, Carrie, and their beautiful families. Thank you for letting me document your lives alongside mine!

To my Faith Center family, who also sometimes find their way onto my scrapbook pages. Thank you for getting excited about my work and giving me the blessing to pursue God's calling on my life. I am richly blessed because of all of you.

To my sweet editor, Kristin Boys, who has been a huge source of help during this journey. Thank you for being an "idea bouncer." I so appreciate the time you've spent helping me work out the map of this book during the writing process. Otherwise, I'd be a busy, frazzled mess!

And to my grandpa, Roger Bivins, who I always thought dropped just a tiny bit of his artistic ability in my lap on his way to heaven. I'm nowhere near your equal, Grandpa, but I think a lot of this passion comes from you!

Memo
page 6

1 Getting Started

page 8

2 Making Art Fast

page 18

3 Preventing Madness

page 42

4 *Using What You've Got*

page 70

5 *Getting Tech Savvy*

page 86

6 *Finding Inspiration*

page 104

Supply Lists 120

Source Guide 124

Index 128

Memo

To: Busy Scrapper
From: Courtney Walsh
Re: Making the Most of Your Scrapbooking Time

Let me guess: You're out running errands and this book begged you to pick it up. You don't really have time to stop and look because you still have to (this part is multiple choice):

a. Finish important paperwork and try to find time to scarf down a sandwich before going back to work for the afternoon and evening.

b. Pick up groceries so you can run home and hope to get dinner made in time, bathe the kids, do homework and get everyone in bed at a decent hour.

c. Run from class to work to the library to your study group, only to finally hit the pillow well after midnight and dream of equations or the English paper you didn't quite finish.

d. Leisurely stroll into your favorite spa for a massage, and then head out for a delicious meal with your girlfriends and a relaxing night at the movies. (Yeah, right.)

Am I close? We live in a world where we have to schedule time for ourselves. Ironically, as soon as I started working on this book, my life picked up pace in astronomical ways. As if getting our house ready to sell, having a baby during the holidays and then moving into our new house were not stressful enough, I was also trying to help my husband with his ministry, write the church newsletter and keep up with my assignments as a contributing editor to *Memory Makers* magazine.

I. Was. Busy.

And so are you! I know. And I'd love to tell you that in this book you'll find all the answers to make albums magically appear on your shelves, but I would be lying—and, well, Mama always said I should tell the truth. Instead, I'll provide you with tips for making the whole process quicker and more enjoyable. Completed albums aren't just a distant dream!

Sincerely,
Courtney

1 Getting Started

Life is busy. I get it. I understand because so often when I bring up scrapbooking to non-scrapbookers they look at me like I'm crazy. "I don't have time to do that!" they say, exasperated. Even seasoned scrapbookers find it hard to keep up with their albums. So I know you're probably itching to find out just how to make some quick layouts.

But hold on a minute. Your frustration with the time you spend scrapbooking isn't just about taking too long to create a page or not finding enough time to sit down in the first place. Your scrap space and the supplies you have on hand play a big part in how fast you scrap—and with how much frustration. So before you dive into some super fast scrapping, spend a few minutes taking stock. Whittle your stash down to the basics that will help you scrap without hassle. Then organize that stash in a way that makes it quick and simple to locate what you need.

I promise, you won't regret not scrapping just yet.

Taking Stock of Supplies

I often say if you create an album with just a photo and a few sentences about what's going on in that photo, then you're scrapbooking. Of course, nowadays, with the growing number of supplies available, it's easy to elaborate on that simple concept. But the number of supplies also means it's easy for the scrapping process to take a lot of time. Sure you can choose to spend hours getting fancy with your pages. But if you want to do some fast and not-so-furious scrapping, you need to narrow down your stash of supplies and stick to the basics.

Cardstock

There are so many different kinds of cardstocks out there in every possible color you can imagine. From textured to smooth to metallic, these solid-colored papers provide your layout with the sturdy background it needs to withstand all the hands that are going to touch it once it's found a home in an album. Be sure to keep a good supply of neutral-color cardstock—like tan, black and white—so you're never left taking time to search for the perfect color.

Patterned Paper

We all have our favorites, and with so many choices out there, it's not difficult to stockpile patterned paper. One of the most important additions to your scrapbook stash, patterned paper is a versatile product that will breathe life into your pages every time! There's no easier way to match paper than with patterns from the same collection. Be sure to store together patterns that coordinate so you can find the right ones in a flash.

Writing Tools

Markers, pens and pencils are all important items to have on hand when starting a scrapbooking project. Handwriting on your layouts is a quick way to get the story on the page, and there are countless utensils to make this process easy! Markers give you the option of adding color to hand-drawn elements, and pencils are a great way to make notes and sketch layouts. And that eraser comes in awfully handy!

Embellishments

Adding accessories to a page—this is the fun part of scrapbooking, don't you think? The decoration of your pages isn't, of course, a necessity, but it certainly adds to the end result. Even a small supply of these products can be a great resource to help you on your way to your best scrapbook pages! But keep in mind that the more embellishments you have, the longer the decision-making will take. Keep your supply of elements to the basics—brads, ribbon, letter stickers, some chipboard—in colors and designs that coordinate with papers you already have.

Cutting Tools

Paper trimmers are a must-have in the world of scrapbooking. Sure, you can cut paper with scissors, but a paper trimmer cuts a straight line in one second flat! Do keep micro-tip scissors on hand for cutting out small elements. A good pair can be worth their weight in gold! Buying a few basic punches—like hole, circle and square shapes—will make creating your own embellishments a breeze. These are investments worth making considering the mileage you're going to get out of each item!

Adhesives

Whether you prefer glue sticks, tape runners, liquid glue or something else entirely, finding a good, reliable adhesive is extremely important to scrapping quickly and easily. And so is keeping a large supply on hand so you don't run out. Eliminate time redoing pages that have fallen apart by ensuring your adhesive is dependable. You might try a few different brands before you finally settle on one that is quick and easy to use. Whatever type you choose, adhesive is one of those supplies you won't be able to scrap without!

Albums

Albums certainly won't help you scrap faster, but they provide great motivation for it! There are so many types of albums just waiting to house your beautiful scrapbooking creations. Choosing among post-bound to spiral-bound and everything in between to find the album that works best for you may take a little shopping around. But to save some time, before you start shopping think about how you want to store your pages and how you want to organize them. Do you want one for each child? One for each year? What system is going to work best for you? Once you figure that out, determine the size you want and start hunting!

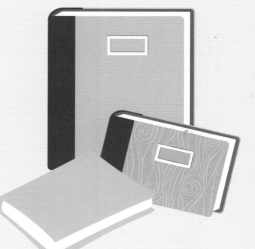

Getting Organized

Believe it or not, one of the quickest ways to waste time is to struggle to find what you're looking for. So now that you've spent some time purging your scrap supply and creating a good stash of materials and tools for easier scrapping, it's time to find a home for everything. With everything in its place, you will save tons of time. Plus, your room will look so much nicer! Ultimately, the best organizational supplies are the ones that work for you and your scrapping style, but the following are my personal favorites for storing tools or supplies.

Storing Paper

One of the simplest ways to keep your cardstock and patterned paper from taking over your entire scrap room is to store it in nifty vertical paper files you can find at craft stores. My favorites are from Cropper Hopper. With the paper standing up, it's easy to flip through. It's best to have at least a few different files if you have a lot of paper. Try organizing by color, by manufacturer or by theme. Hanging file folders are another great way to get a bird's-eye view of your entire collection, making it super simple to pull out just what you need.

Toting Tools

Keep those often-used tools like rulers, pens and pencils, hole punches and scissors at arm's length by storing them where you can see them—on top of your desk. You can invest in a pretty scrapbooking desktop caddy, but toolboxes and even empty coffee cans will help you organize as well. The key is to house the tools so you can see them and put them right back in their place when you're done.

Rounding Up Ribbon

Storing your ribbon in a see-through jar not only makes for a beautiful array of color on your shelf, but also for a quick find when you need that perfect trim! Inexpensive jars can be found at craft stores, but you can use clean spaghetti sauce jars as well. Organizing jars by ribbon color or type of trim will go a long way toward saving your sanity.

Containing Adhesives

A basket on top of your desk or a drawer dedicated to adhesives is one option that is bound to save you time. You can also store a basket full of adhesive in a drawer so it's quick to take out and also quick to put away. Adhesive is one of the most essential, can't-live-without-it things in your scrap stash, so it makes sense to keep it quick to find.

Corralling Small Embellishments

Buttons, brads, eyelets and beads: They're so tiny and so easy to lose, what's a busy scrapper to do? Don't despair! Anything compartmentalized into tiny sections—like containers intended for jewelry or small hardware—is perfect storage. Consider making use of old containers like empty baby food jars or spice jars. Organize containers by the type of embellishment for easy selection.

Organizing Sheets of Embellishments

It's handy that embellishments like stickers, alphas, chipboard and rub-ons come in sheets, so everything's together. But it's not convenient when you start to cut your sheet of rub-ons or when you've amassed a pile of stickers. Simple binders with page protectors are great storage options for these unruly sheets. Keeping a sheet or two in one clear page protector makes it easy to flip through your entire collection and corral any loose pieces.

Collecting Punches and Other Bulky Materials

Some supplies don't fit nicely into file folders or empty cans. Punches, especially, with their awkward shapes and hefty sizes, present an organizational obstacle. If you have an empty wall or closet shelf, line up a couple baskets and put your punches right in. Remember that carrying around a basketful of punches isn't all that practical, so you might want to keep your most-used shapes close by. Baskets are great catchalls for all kinds of bulky supplies like stamps, ink pads and paint bottles.

Sorting Photos

We all have boxes and boxes of photos, most of which are disorganized and confusing! It's not going to be a small task, but going through these pictures and categorizing them will eventually make your life a lot easier! Break pictures down chronologically, then sort them into tabbed photo boxes or files for quick, easy access. If you're accumulating digital photographs, categorize your photos in a similar way. For instance, create a 2008 folder on your hard drive and add subfolders organized by theme or month. It's up to you exactly how you do it, but find a system that works and stick to it!

Keeping Works-in-Progress

It happens to all of us. We're in the middle of a layout when the water boils over, the baby starts crying or you realize you're late for a meeting. Rather than pack everything up, forcing you to start over again tomorrow, Basic-Grey's handy magnetic mat allows you to stick everything in place without committing to anything on a whim. A clear pocket like the ones from Cropper Hopper is also a great way to keep supplies for one layout together. You can even use clean, empty pizza boxes to store unfinished layouts. Whatever you choose, the next chance you have to get back to work, you can dive right in.

2 *Making Art Fast*

The best way to enjoy scrapbooking in spite of your busy schedule is to figure out as many ways as possible to scrapbook quickly. I used to spend hours on my pages. I would choose photos and then proceed to drag every product I owned onto my table. Considering how indecisive I am, this only slowed me down. Slow and steady, but I wasn't winning any races!

After each child's birth, I picked up more ways to create my pages quickly. But that didn't mean I stopped enjoying the process; in fact, quite the opposite happened. I now feel liberated in my newfound ability to work quickly, and getting my pages done no longer feels like a burden. With just a few simple strategies, you can learn to work at record speed, too. This chapter is all about shortcuts. Read on for ways to get it done!

Use Less Stuff

Here's an idea: Put fewer elements on your pages. You'll not only speed up your process, your purchases will stretch a lot farther, and your pages will look a lot cleaner. This layout uses only cardstock, patterned paper, a chipboard leaf, letters and a button. Surprisingly, I don't feel like it's missing anything. And it sure was quick to finish!

When the heat of summer finally subsides, we are always ready to welcome the fall. And one of our favorite things is playing at the park. You just can't beat these kinds of days!

fall fun

christmas 2007

cannot get over how beautiful you are, Sophia! '07

Try a Smaller Size

If you want to make scrapping quicker, try a smaller page size. This layout is actually 8" x 8" (20cm x 20cm), and it came together at lightning speed! With smaller pages, there's not as much space to fill, and small photos become more than enough for a page. Isn't a small completed book better than an empty large album?

Don't Line Up Everything

I have nothing against straight lines, but sometimes it's a huge time-saver not to line up everything! I tore these scraps of paper, giving them a soft white edge. I also kept the block of floral paper in the size I found it, and adhered it at a slightly crooked angle. It's larger than my background sheet, but I love the way it looks.

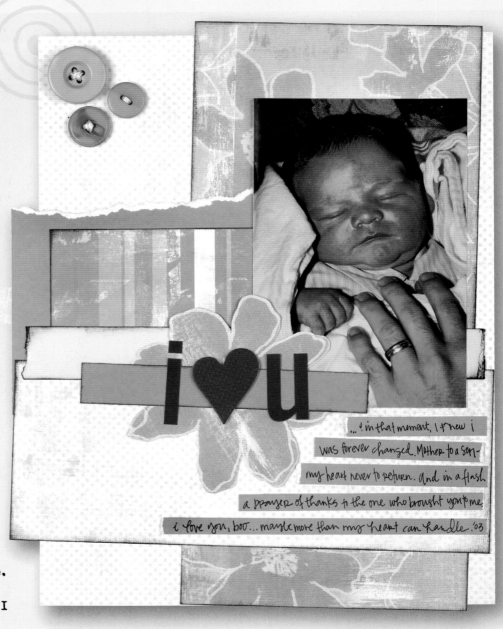

i ♥ u

... & in that moment, I knew i was forever changed. Mother to a son— my heart never to return. And in a flash a prayer of thanks to the one who brought you to me i love you, boo... maybe more than my heart can handle. '03

laugh
6 2 7 4 3 5 1 9 6 2 7 4 3
i don't laugh enough. It's because of my teeth. Those dang eye teeth. that & the fact that you can see my gums. how stupid is that? who cares!? I need to laugh MORE.

Add Large Embellishments

Do you ever get in the mood to just be creative ... fast! That's how I felt when I sat down to make this layout. The photo was leftover from a mini album, and the scraps were scattered on my desk. I just started gluing and ended up with this simple layout. Plus, using a large embellishment made a big impact in a flash!

Handwrite Your Words ➜

You can find all kinds of ways to document the stories behind the photos, but one of the quickest is to use your own handwriting instead of typing and printing out the words. It's even quicker to write directly on your background paper rather than worrying about finding and attaching a separate journaling block. Plus, handwriting lends a personal charm.

Skip Long-Winded Journaling

My mom told me, "Not everyone wants to read a novel for every photo." Point taken. And, really, who has the time to write one? Sometimes you can say what you're thinking in just a sentence or two. Next time you're journaling, try to come up with a concise yet effective way to get your sentiments across.

i wish

I could freeze time just for a little while...

because you, Sophia, are growing up way too fast.

Little swimmer

GIGGLE & SMILE

DELIGHT

at the beginning of the
summer, Sophia wouldn't go

near the water alone. Floaties &
a life vest didn't help at all...

it wasn't until miss Carla gave
her a swim lesson that she

finally started getting comfort
able in the water. By the

time summer ended, she was in
the deep end cruising like a pro!

Embellish with Stickers

I remember a time when I thought in order for a page to be complete I had to labor over it for hours. Obviously, that got really old really fast. One simple way to streamline your process is to stop using complicated or handcut titles. Decorative stickers are so easy to apply that they're the perfect solution to save you time without sacrificing a beautiful layout!

Kelly Goree
cleans up her space

Busy Scrapper

When life gets busy I try to do all I can to keep on scrapping! My number-one way to save time is to keep my space cleaned up and cleared out after each project. It takes a little time after each project but saves lots of time in the long run. I also keep an item or two on my desk that inspires me— from a photo to a new product to an idea in a magazine. And I have no problem using sketches as a way to stir my creative juices when none of my own seem to be going anywhere. I either use my own sketches or one from the infinite variety of cool sketch sites on the Web.

Artwork by Kelly Goree

Leave Chipboard Undressed

Who doesn't love chipboard? One of the most versatile and easy-to-use products on the market, chipboard offers endless possibilities. Paint it, sand it, ink it or save yourself the time and leave it raw like Kelly did here. Rough chipboard makes a great complement to this layout about football. Sometimes, things are absolutely perfect even without any finishing touches!

SUMMER 2006

HAPPY! Plans Sunshine Water Hot! Swimming Laugh JOY tons of fun! WET!

#1 Way to Make Art Fast

Be a planner!

If most of your scrapping time is spent moving elements around, sketch layouts in advance. If you struggle with journaling, jot down a few words before you store away photos; you'll have journaling ready when you need it. If you waste time searching for embellishments, make your own "kits"—a couple papers and embellishments to match—and grab one before you begin. Thinking ahead will reward you with so much more time!

Let a Photo Be the Background

I love patterned paper as much as the next guy, but every now and then, I have a photo that deserves to stand alone. So why not supersize a picture and embellish right on it? For this layout, some strategically placed flowers and felt flourishes kept my layout from being plain, but the photo is the star of this page!

thankful

for your sweet side... the one that always makes me smile.

Use One Large Photo

Make life a little easier and focus on using just one large photo on your next layout. There are no decisions about focal points and how to arrange all the photos in a pleasing manner. Keep the embellishments simple and minimal, and you'll finish a layout in no time!

Artwork by Heather Burch

Make Adhesive Dots Your Friends

Buttons are, hands down, some of my favorite embellishments. From the looks of it, Heather feels the same! Rather than hand-sewing these buttons to her page (a process that can be very long and tedious), Heather used adhesive dots for a quick application. The results are no less beautiful ... just far less time consuming!

TREE climber

There you are again: eyes sparkling and curious with adventure.

The trees in the yard seem to hold secrets for you to find. You like to look down at the world around you and capture it in your hand.

I sometimes wonder if you have something hidden up there that calls to you. Then I remember that you told me once, "it's like a secret spot where I can go when I want to be alone and just watch everything."

A place to be alone with your thoughts, your dreams, and your imagination.

Of course, it's surely another great reason that God gave us trees.

2007

Artwork by Linda Albrecht

Give Transparencies a Try

This layout looks complicated, but Linda promises it was quick to make! The pieces of transparencies she included (the black flourishes) add detail and dimension that didn't take a lot of time to create. Next time you're looking for a unique but simple detail, why not give transparencies a try?

birthday BOY

This year, your grandparents were going to be out of town on your actual birthday, so we held a little impromptu party for you about a week early. But even a spur-of-the-moment bash couldn't be complete without a birthday cake and candles! You had such a good time blowing them out you're an old pro at four years old now that we even did it a second time just to squeeze out one more wish! Happy Birthday, my monkey boy...may all your wishes come true! August 19, 2007

make a WISH

Artwork by Kelly Goree

Personalize with Hand-Drawn Details

Page kits are a great basis for quick layouts. But even if you want to be quick, you don't have to sacrifice creativity by using only the kit. Add your own touch, as Kelly did here with hand-drawn details. They're personal and unique, plus, hand-drawn elements aren't meant to be perfect, saving you even more time.

Scrap Photos Right Now ➜

A surefire way to make a quick layout is to scrap the photos on the
day you take them. The thoughts are still fresh, and the story is
easy to capture. You won't struggle with what to say, and odds are,
since the pictures are so new, you'll be inspired to knock out a
layout in no time!

LAUGHTER is the shortest distance between 2 people

Make a Statement

Sometimes the easiest way to make a statement is to allow a quote to speak all by itself. To really let the words take center stage, you can mix and match large letters on a simple background. Using lots of large letters is a great way to fill space and create a bold design quickly and easily.

...In so many ways, it still feels like

H O M E

My parents house is so homey & relaxing. how could a part of me NOT consider it home? the little details all over make-this house unique. From the photos everywhere, to the teddy bears my mom used to collect to this awesome type-writer I found at a flea market, but had no spot for...this house is my safe haven - so many great memories in these 4 walls.

Leave Journaling for Later

Coming up with what to say sometimes takes the biggest chunk of scrapping time. If you're stumped for words, create a layout without journaling. Then use a photo to create a journaling pocket by attaching the sides and bottom to the page. Insert a blank piece of paper with a tab and add journaling later.

'05

l o v e my BOY

the sweetest BOY. cuddly. Happy. Funny. ALL BOY. I ♡ U.

Kick-Start Challenge

Challenges are great for jump-starting our creative juices and getting us scrapping fast. Try this challenge to start:

Pick out five products and use only those five things on a page. You may worry you're limiting yourself, but in reality, by focusing on just a few elements, you're likely to activate your creativity. Plus, you'll eliminate the time-consuming task of making decisions.

Punch out Unique Details

Adding unusual details to a page doesn't require a lot of work; something quick and simple can do the trick. Use a circular punch to create a large hole inside a picture and you've got the perfect spot to record the date. It's a quick touch that gives this page a punch of extraordinary.

hopscotch

I went away for the day one Saturday, leaving the kids with Paul for the day. When I came home the footpath was covered in chalk drawings and my camera had these pics on it. Abby at 3 ½ years old, discovering hopscotch with Isobel.
June 7th 2007.

Artwork by Nic Howard

Ink Photo Edges

If you're looking for a quick way to make your photos pop off the page, try inking the edges like Nic did here. We regularly ink cardstock, patterned paper, even chipboard. So why not take the ink pad directly to the most important part of the layout ... the pictures? It gives your page a power-packed punch, and eliminates the need to spend time hand-cutting photo mats.

Be a Multitasker

The easiest way to scrap in a flash is to do two things at once. One quick and simple way to add the story to your page is to handwrite journaling on a die-cut embellishment. Die-cuts and stickers like these add color and interest while providing a place for your words to rest.

SOLID.

You are so safe for me. So solid. Such a firm foundation we've built our relationship on...I feel so fortunate to be married to someone like you. You're constantly looking for ways to make my life easier, selfless like no one else I know. Even when we're arguing, it seems this solid foundation is always there. I thank God for you every single day.

Apply Blocks of Pattern

Add blocks of pattern in varying sizes to your next layout, and you'll find the design comes together quickly. Pretty patterns can stand on their own, eliminating the need for much embellishment. And using blocks makes building a simple design around rectangular photos a snap. Add a title and journaling and voila!—another completed page.

Holding on a little tighter to Daddy as you were feeling a bit shy and unsure of the situation.

feeling **SHY**

Artwork by Greta Hammond

Timesaving Tools
Die-Cutting Machines

Making art quickly is a must for the busy scrapper, and one way to do that is to invest in a die-cutting machine. These machines, like Provo Craft's Cricut and the QuicKutz family of tools, are easy to use, and the results are clean and pristine every time! You can create titles, subtitles and die-cuts in just about every shape, font and color you want! What could be quicker (and easier) than that?

Say Good-Bye to Hand-Cutting

Typically, I'm not great with new machines. But I now realize I could be saving so much time using a handy die-cutting machine. Greta's title looks intricately hand-cut, but her machine did all the work! While it may seem daunting, once you start using a new machine, you're sure to rely on it again and again!

"Mom, can we get one?" was all I heard when Uncle Matt and Aunt Carrie showed up with their brand new bull dog puppy, Boss.

While I believe there is some truth to the thought that every little boy needs a dog... my answer didn't require much thought.

"Not a chance," I said firmly. "But you can play with Boss any time you want to!

"Stitch" with Rub-Ons

I've got a confession to make: I can't figure out how to use my sewing machine. You can imagine how happy I was to find a way to get the look of machine stitching without the talent of actually being able to sew! These rub-on stitches are so easy to apply. They're a great way to add that finishing touch with no trouble at all!

3 Preventing Madness

One night, I was working on a layout when everything just went wrong. My adhesive stuck to the wrong part of the paper, tearing it and making it unusable. My brad was already stuck through the layout, but when I pulled the prongs down I realized it wasn't even near the spot I had intended. These annoyances were starting to get to me, and I believe my exact words were, "Aarrggghhh!"

"Are you always like this when you scrapbook?" my husband asked from his safe spot on the other side of the room. I shot him a dirty look. "I'm just saying," he said. "I thought it was supposed to be fun."

He had a point: It *was* supposed to be fun. It was then I started realizing how desperately I needed to employ a few methods to prevent madness. Whenever your stress is getting the best of you, you might be able to utilize some of these tips yourself!

Artwork by Heather Burch

Keep It Simple

One of my favorite ways to lay out photos is straight across the page.
So simple! Just plop them down and build the design around them.
However, when that gets stale, try mixing it up by giving one photo
a different treatment, like making it bigger or adding a frame like
Heather did. Popping it out a little provides an instant focal point.

Frame Photos with Trim

Set your focal photo apart from the others by creating an easy photo frame out of ribbon, rickrack, fabric or any other kind of trim. You can staple it into place, use regular adhesive or apply adhesive dots for a fast, easy element that leads the eye directly where you want it to go!

Purchase Product Lines

One of the best-ever scrapbooking ideas is coordinating product lines. It's so easy to stroll down the aisle at your local scrapbook store and pick up a few sheets of coordinating patterned paper. And, oh, look! There are even some stickers and chipboard and a few other fun embellishments that work perfectly with the paper! Picking up matching favorites takes away all of the guesswork.

Kick-Start Challenge

If you're tired of searching for adhesive, hunting for perfect papers and tracking down that decorative punch, try this challenge: Grab some photos from your pile. Go over to your desk and sit down.

Scrap a page using only products that are currently within arm's reach.

No moving from your chair (unless, of course, you have to use the bathroom!). No adhesive? Try a stapler! Mismatched product? Use it in small doses for a quilted look.

There are a couple of years between the two of you, but there seems to be this little bond forming. Really. It's just too cute.

UNLIKELY PAIR. THE 2 OF YOU.

Artwork by Heather Burch

Join a Kit Club

For Heather, owner of Poppy Ink, the benefits of a kit club are obvious. If you have trouble mixing and matching patterns and products from various lines and manufacturers, don't stress about it—join a kit club and let someone else do it for you! Kit clubs send you a great assortment of products like the ones on this layout. Mix and match without any effort on your part!

cute

a bundle of joy

Sept 11, 2007
almost 2 months old

Lily

You have only been a part of our family for a short time – and we already can't imagine life without you! As the fourth child, you get lots of love and attention. I love to hold you as much as I can. It is such a treat to have a tiny baby in our home again. I am trying to make the most of these precious days, because I know how fast you will grow and change! For now, I am going to spend every minute I can memorizing your sweet little face.

our sweet baby girl

Artwork by Brenda Carpenter

Stick to Similar Hues

Mixing colors can be part of the fun of scrapbooking, but it can also be part of the frustration. Next time you're struggling to find colors that go together perfectly, consider a monochromatic page like Brenda's. Sticking with pink (and a bit of white) allowed her to create an adorable layout perfectly suited for a baby girl.

i am so glad our kids are close with my parents. Having a good relationship with grandparents is so important to me... and our kids hit the jackpot! this is one relationship to treasure forever! Dani {2006}

Fake the Look of Brads

If you're like me, you love the added punch that brads can bring to a page. But brads can also be a big pain, what with all the piercing and sticking your fingernail in to open up the prongs. Plus, I find once they're in, they aren't exactly where I wanted them (argh ...). No more! These dot stickers, found at any office supply store, are a great alternative to brads—and without the hassle!

...but i wanted to win!

Okay, this is obviously something we need to work on with you.

Losing is definitely not something you're very good at. This little meltdown came after you and Sophia raced across the field at the church and she arrived at the finish line before you.

How am I going to help you learn it doesn't matter if you win every time... as long as you do your best?

I'm not sure... but we're working on it!

Rethink Adhesive Application ➔

I love the way individual words assembled together look on a layout. It gives your journaling a punch. But seriously, who has the patience to add adhesive to all those little words? Instead, put adhesive on the entire journaling block and then cut the journaling into pieces. This makes the entire process much simpler.

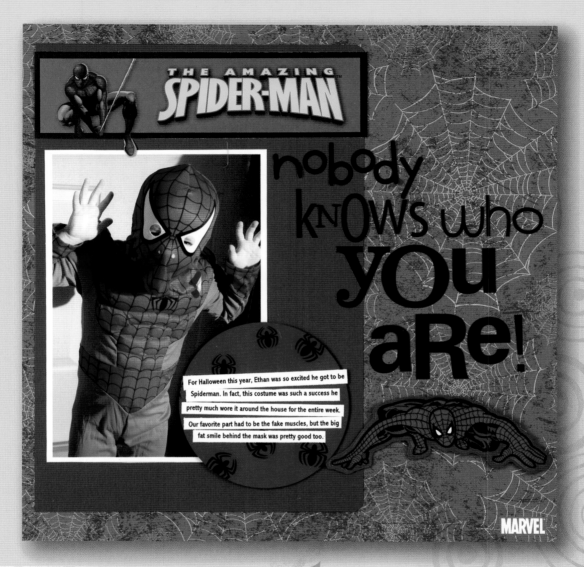

For Halloween this year, Ethan was so excited he got to be Spiderman. In fact, this costume was such a success he pretty much wore it around the house for the entire week. Our favorite part had to be the fake muscles, but the big fat smile behind the mask was pretty good too.

Mix and Match Letters

If there's one thing I love, it's letter stickers. I have a little bit of an obsession, actually, so you can imagine how frustrating it is to have sheets of mostly used letters. Next time you can't make a single word with any one sheet of stickers, just mix and match them! There's nothing wrong with a little variety.

Think Outside the Box

Don't you hate it when you attach your title letters only to find out that you're one sticker short? When I discovered a missing T for this title, I simply layered an F over an upside-down L and trimmed away the excess. If I hadn't mentioned it, would you have known? With a little thought, it's easy to find creative solutions and avoid frustration.

Laughter... is the fulfillment of happiness... and what mothers hope and dream for their children. How blessed I truly feel to see the laughter between you

Artwork by Linda Albrecht

Keep Letters Handy

When I found out Linda scrapbooks in the car while waiting to pick up her son, I realized this was a woman who knew how to get things done! One of her best tips is to print out a page of letters of varying fonts and sizes and keeping it handy. It's an easy way to add words to layouts when you don't have a printer at your disposal.

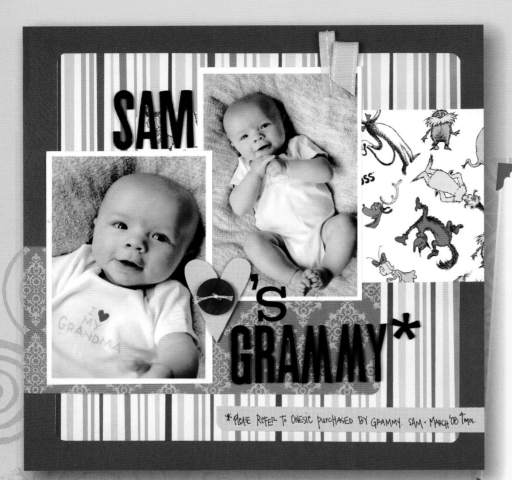

#1 Way to Prevent Madness

Keep it simple!

It may sound obvious, but using letter stickers instead of hand-cutting, inking photo edges instead of cutting a mat, and skipping the eyelets altogether will make the scrapping process breezier. The fewer steps you take, the less hassle you'll end up dealing with. Keeping it simple will help you focus on, and enjoy, your scrapping time rather than dread it.

Round Those Corners

A corner rounder enables you to make a page look "done" with ease. Rounded corners—whether on paper, like I did on this layout, or on photos—give any square a nice, finished edge that doesn't require additional detail to look complete. One easy punch and you're done!

Artwork by Brenda Carpenter

Create Monthly Layouts

Take the pressure off scrapping every single photo by creating one layout for each month. Brenda's layout is a compilation of important memories from October. While she has several other scrap-worthy pictures from that month, getting the highlights down releases the guilt of needing to "catch up." Follow the same sketch each month to save yourself time.

Stick with Borders

It's possible to add funky patterns to a page without dipping into your stash of paper! Incorporating border stickers, which are self-adhesive, helped me create a bright background without any problem! This layout was a cinch to create, and with all the patterns out there, you could repeat this idea over and over and never have two layouts turn out alike!

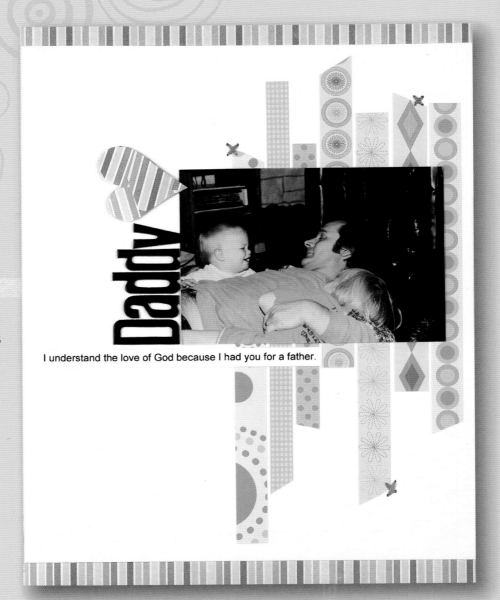

Daddy

I understand the love of God because I had you for a father.

The two of you exuded happiness as you bounded your way up the hill.

Your little legs burst with energy and left me trailing behind.

It was a beautiful summer day, with nothing but blues skies ahead.

And when you finally reached your destination, you felt as though you were on top of the world!

ON top OF THE world

so happy together so happy together so happy

Artwork by Greta Hammond

Use Neutrals

To avoid a lot of confusion and hassle, Greta often relies on neutral-colored backgrounds. "It saves time not having to go through stacks of colors trying to find the perfect one," she says. "And those neutral colors allow your photos to shine." Black, brown, white or cream backgrounds are great ways to make other colors pop right off the page.

Pick a Theme

When I saw these
papers, I instantly
remembered photos
of my daughter
sporting pirate gear. In this case, the product
determined the theme of the layout. It's OK to
create a layout simply because you like the papers
you see in the store. It saves you time and effort
in the long run; odds are, if the product inspires
the idea, the creativity will come easily.

The scrapbook layout includes the following journaling text:

Getting Sophia to clean up her room is more than a chore, it's a pain in the butt.

I told her to get upstairs and pick it up which brought on the whining...

"But it's TOO MESSY!"

I said, "If you would put stuff away when you're done with it, your room wouldn't look like that."

She said, "I know, but I just have

SUCH A BIG IMAGINATION!"

She gets points for originality... but they're negated by the piles on her floor.

Don't Pigeonhole Product

At the same time, you don't need to reserve themed products, like my pirate paper, for the theme for which they're intended. Odds are, within the themed collection, there are a few papers general enough to use on any layout. Don't pigeonhole a product: Look to the patterns and colors, and you'll likely be inspired to use papers in an entirely new way!

find **something**

in **every day** that

makes you

smile

- Kobi Yamada

Artwork by Brenda Carpenter

Assemble Your Own Kit

Next time you're going to a crop, put together your own page kit like Brenda did for this layout here. The initial time investment will more than pay for itself once you arrive with everything you need to create two or three pages as soon as you sit down! It will also save you the hassle of hauling everything you own back and forth to the crop.

little pool...
big
fun
2007

Skip the Journaling

Sometimes, it's OK not to journal. (Gasp!) Of course, the point of scrapbooking is to preserve memories, but you can save yourself the pressure of finding the right words by letting some photos speak for themselves. It's obvious what's going on in these pictures, so I just added a title, recorded the date and had a completed page.

Use Chipboard Die-Cuts

I stumbled upon the fact that companies are creating beautiful die-cuts to overlay chipboard, saving me the hassle of painting, inking or otherwise altering chipboard to suit my needs. All I had to do to create these 3-D goodies was punch the die-cut away from the background and glue it to the chipboard. As my daughter would say, "Easy peasy, lemon squeezy!"

Make a
Bonus Project

I had all of the tools and supplies leftover from "Brilliantly Simple" (on the previous page) sitting on my desk, so I decided to put them to good use. Using just the leftovers, I created a handmade card in minutes! Even if you don't need a card for any reason, you'll save frustration later when there's no need for last-minute scrambling.

little
fun & fabulous
**fall
frolic**

November 2007

What a day we had. Mama got you from school and we decided to grab lunch out since it was such a gorgeous fall day. On our way back home we saw these huge piles of leaves on Main Street so of course we stopped to play! What a sight to see you make the leaves fly!

Artwork by Kelly Goree

Start with a Plan

Figuring out the general layout of a page before you begin is a great, easy way to save yourself time. After first creating this quick digital template, Kelly was able to attack her page with a plan. Her pieces were already laid out for her, making the actual design a snap! For a kick start, create your own page based on Kelly's sketch (below).

2x3" photo | 2x3" photo | 2x3" photo | **Title**
2x3" photo | 2x3" photo | 3.5 x 5" photo
embellie

I'm going to go ahead and embrace 35 years old.

Well I have no choice really.

After years of telling people I was 5 years younger than I really am.

I was sung 'Happy Birthday' by 150 people at a conference recently.

After it was announced it was my 35th birthday.

Such a surprise to those that attended my 30th party last year...

Artwork by Nic Howard

Focus Your Embellishments

Are you ever stumped about where to put your embellishments? Nic saves lots of guesswork by building the bulk of her elements in the same area. Here, she added several embellishments to the left of the photo, allowing her to focus her energy on that one spot. With a concentrated grouping, you get a great finished look in half the time!

Snap Photos of Signs

Pressed for time? Out of alphas? Stumped about how to make the
title? Have no fear! When you're out and about, take photos of the
signs around you. It'll not only help you remember what your photos
are all about, but you can cut out a sign and use that as your title.

Everyday, Sophia wants to know if she can paint. With real paints. She loves to create her mini works of art and then loves to give them as gifts. This is such a part of our day - you painting or drawing, me writing or working... hanging out. I love that you are creative and that I have the opportunity to allow you to freely explore the fun of art. I love that most afternoons, it's you and me, babe. Playing and pretending to be artists. I'm having so much fun!

BuddingArtist

Ink Paper Edges

There are so many easy and fabulous ways to add detail without any effort at all! I love to ink the edges of pieces of paper before attaching them to a page. And tearing edges before inking adds even more texture and dimension in seconds. To make inking nice and pretty, gently brush a small ink pad along the edges. And neatness doesn't count!

Virginia Williams
puts her workspace out of reach

One of the best things I ever did was move the height of my desk up to countertop height. Before, I was always packing things away so little hands wouldn't disturb the layout I currently had in progress. After moving my table up, I found I could leave my layouts out when I wasn't working on them. That way I could spend five minutes here or 10 minutes there, and eventually I'd complete a layout using only a few stolen moments out of the craziness of my life. If I waited until I had a solid block of time to work, I would never have finished layouts!

The making of

A Home Run

1 Step 1: Have daddy show you how to hold the bat.

2 Step 2: Take your stance and aim.

3 Step 3: Swing! Great job Ty, you hit it! It didn't get too far, but not bad for a first try!

Well Almost

I'm glad you liked you birthday present from daddy Ty! He sure had fun teaching you how to use it! Ty's birthday 11-06.

Artwork by Virginia Williams

Just Grab and Go

You could easily spend all your time looking for a picture to scrap. Or you could start flipping through the pile and stop at the first one(s) that catch your eye. Virginia passed over these photos several times, sure she didn't have the "perfect" papers to complement them. This time, she avoided frustration by refusing to stew over it. She just grabbed the first thing and went for it!

There's no doubt you love getting a trophy – a fitting reward for a season of hard work (ok - so some days you were harder working than others, but still!) It was a great season & we were so proud.!

SOCCER

07

Artwork by Kelly Goree

Scrap Standard-Sized Prints

Don't have the energy to hassle with sizing and resizing photos on the computer? No problem! Focus on those 4" x 6" (10cm x 15cm) prints you pick up from the photo processor! There's no need to enlarge or shrink a great photograph, as you can see in Kelly's layout. Simply choose your favorites and start building a page.

4 Using What You've Got

We've all got one. I mean, we are, after all, scrapbookers. You know what I'm talking about: the stash of stuff. We buy, we hoard, we keep everything. From scraps and leftovers, to cardboard boxes and catalogs, to tons of other craft supplies, we always think in the back of our minds, "What if I can use this someday?"

While I am all for purging clutter out of your life, I also think that often using what you already have can be the perfect addition to a layout. You don't have to take time running all over town looking for the perfect supplies. You don't have to stage a photo shoot. You don't even have to use scrapbooking stuff. Just look around! Read on for some interesting ways to use what you've got.

Ever since your sister started school,
You've been ready for your turn!
Don't worry, Ethan, it'll be here soon enough!
And you're going to have so much fun!

SChOOL DAyS

Color a Page with Scraps

Small scraps strategically place on a layout can be just the punc of color your page needs. On thi page, I've incorporated several stray pieces of patterned paper I had lying around. These small pieces paired with other small pieces make a big statement.

Kendall came with the older girls to the
Princess Party, and she had no trouble
at all stepping into her role as Queen
Bee. Gotta love a princess with attitude!

Be a Graphic Artist

Just because you use scraps doesn't mean they have to look like scraps. Cut pieces all to the same size for a neat and tidy, graphic look. Plus, using squares of patterned paper is an easy way to create a fabulous background for your page, especially if you have only smaller photos to scrap.

Oh, wow, do I know this walk. Sassy Miss Sophia has got quite a little attitude every now and then. You know, it should probably upset me, and sometimes - depending on how far she tries to take it, it does. But on this particular day, trying to get her to leave the ball field... I just had to laugh. Her tiny little butt was shaking in full force as she gave me the hair flip and sassed herself away. Granted, she got a good talking-to... but not until *after* I got this photo. It still makes me smile.

SASS

Sophia...testing her mother and exercising her indpendence.

Add Detail with Ribbon Scraps

You know by now that using scraps makes scrapping fast. But don't just stick to paper scraps. Here, I turned to some of my smallest ribbon scraps to add a little detail. Then I broke out a few short strands of floss for some stitching around the page. These little details may not look like much on their own, but they make the layout perfectly complete.

House Journaling in Cards

I'm drawn to the stationery aisle at my local Target. I can't seem to go in without checking out what's new, and I usually find a way to justify buying more stuff. Instead of reserving a stash of adorable stationery for its intended use, use it on your next layout. This card made the perfect house for my journaling, and it added pizzazz to the page.

#1 Way to Use What You've Got

Think outside the scrapbook aisle!

Just because something didn't come from the scrapbook store doesn't mean you use can't use it! Raid your house for potentially unique and fabulous additions to your scrapbook pages. Staples and paper-clips are great substitutes for brads, and bubble wrap makes a unique stamp. Try craft sticks as interesting journaling strips, or mold pipe cleaners into unique embellishments. The possibilities are endless— and right there in front of you!

Make Use of Found Objects

If you're anything like me, it's hard to throw away anything that might make a cool addition to a scrapbook page. Part of my obsession extends to cardboard boxes, like the one I've used here as the background for this layout. Try looking at found objects, like cardboard, as artistic additions to your pages. You just might fall in love with the results.

moments i treasure

changed.

in mamelodi, i learned the true meaning of god's purpose for me. how fortunate i am to learn at such a young age that god has a plan for my life... and that if i let him have control, he will use me to change lives 10,000 miles away from home.

SHE takes care of you...

Sophia is a little mama to you, Ethan. Sometimes that means taking care of you and helping you. Sometimes that means bossing you around and telling you what to do and how to do it.

As you grow, though, there may be times when she's going to need YOU to look out for her. Knowing you and how sweet you already are, I don't think it will be a problem... but I just wanted to remind you... she may be older, but she needs you as much as you need her!

RETURN the favor, ok?

Cut Up Catalogs

I finally found justification for my insane "save everything" mentality. I created this layout using the BasicGrey catalog. I snipped the thumbnails of their new releases and made a mosaic of tiny prints on the background. I didn't measure anything; I simply snipped them as they were, layered them and added a few other elements. The design looks intricate, but there's nothing to it!

Don't Trash Chipboard

You've used up your chipboard shapes and now you're going to throw
the leftover part in the trash. But wait a minute. It's perfectly
good chipboard, easy to paint or alter, and frankly, sometimes
the leftover part—like the arrows here—is even better than the
part you punched out! Next time, before you pitch it, give leftover
chipboard a second look. It might be just the embellishment you
need to make that layout complete.

Sometimes when i watch you at play i like to imagine what you WILL be WHEN YOU GROW UP

I always find it hard to narrow it down to one thing, so I imagine that you will be a master of many things and I will always be there to tell you how brightly you shine.

UNFORGETTABLE

Adore

04102006

Artwork by Linda Albrecht

Busy Scrapper

Recycle Leftovers

Linda could win an award for recycling. On this page, she was able to use leftover chipboard and rub-ons, tiny bits of ribbon and paper scraps! Those little items leftover after you finish a page may fit together perfectly to create a layout of their own. Before you toss the leftovers, give them a second chance to wow you on a page.

Linda Albrecht
sticks to her favorites

I love to do something creative each day, so I have learned that I need to simplify when it comes to scrapbooking. My pages don't reflect a simple style or a lack of embellishments, but I've learned that placing the supplies I use the most within easy reach cuts my work time. I used to spend an hour just going through papers and embellishments, only to find that I stick to a favorite brand or style. So now, all of my very favorite papers are in one paper caddy that sits below my work table, and my favorite letters and rub-ons are right next to them. I can easily grab all the basics and complete a layout in no time.

Scraplift Your Layouts

I loved my layout "Pucker Up" about my niece (above), and I knew I could create another well-designed layout based on the same sketch. Rather than just "lift" the original design, I flipped it. If you turn "Pucker Up" to the right, you'll see the design frame I used for this layout, "True Friend." Flipping is a quick way to use what you have to create layouts with a tried-and-true design.

I have to credit scrapbooking with a lot of happy things in my life, but one of the happiest is my friendship with Leah. Leah is one of the first people I met when I started scrapbooking, and over the years, her friendship has become one of the greatest blessings to me. There's certain people who are just so TRUE in every aspect of their life, and that's Leah. She's a 'man of her word' as she says... and I believe it. I feel like it was divine intervention that we connected first via the internet and then in real life. Though an entire country of land may separate us, our kindred spirits are truly linked. Thank you, Leah, for being such a good friend.

Use What Works

I loved the way the Anna Griffin papers and embellishments worked with my black-and-white photo in "True Friend" (on the previous page). Instead of putting them all away after I finished, I printed another black-and-white photo and created an entirely new layout. I already knew how the elements would work on the page so this layout came together in minutes.

beautiful

i don't think you have any idea how beautiful you are, Sophia. Sometimes, like in this photo, you take my breath away. i pray as you grow older you see yourself through my eyes. I ♥ you. 10·07

Kick-Start Challenge

Whether they're kids' crafts, sewing notions or art supplies, you probably have tons of fun materials you could use on your pages. So, give your layouts a handmade feel!

Try something you've never done.

Use paint, fabric, felt or hand stitching to bring out that unique look only you can create! Give yourself a few minutes to gather supplies and 30 minutes to scrap, and see what kind of masterpiece you come up with.

Button Up Pages

Buttons are so pretty, aren't they? And we all have a stash of them; it's hard to avoid when they come with all our new clothes. Buttons make great embellishments, giving you texture, color and pop all at the same time. The next time you're struggling for the perfect finishing touch, turn to your own stash of buttons or other notions, and you'll be set!

soup

after a few years of enjoying
apple-butternut squash soup from
Whole Foods, this fall I decided
to try making it from scratch.
I haven't done much cooking, but
I found a simple recipe online &
next thing I knew, I had
a big huge pot of the most
DELICIOUS soup ever! It's even
more flavorful than the store bought
version. I am super proud
of my new cooking attempts &
can't wait to make some
soup to share.

102707

homemade

Artwork by Jennifer Pebbles

Stamp Your Art Out

Many people stumble onto scrapbooking thanks to their love of rubber
stamping. Easy, intricate designs are just a stamp away! Jennifer's
layout shows how she used one stamp in three different places to simply
embellish her page. Think about how you can use your own stamps to
quickly add dimension and embellishment.

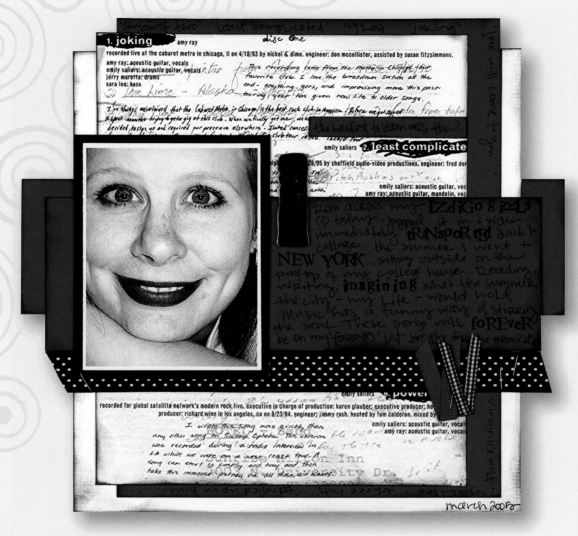

Don't Stress About Photos

Often I'll have a thought I want to capture on a layout for posterity's sake, but I don't have the "right" photo to go along with the story. I could go out and stage a photo shoot or I could simply use a general shot I already have lying around. In this layout, I used an image of myself and the liner notes from one of my CDs.

always

LIFE IS GOOD

8·7·04

Artwork by Jennifer Pebbles

Scrap a Mini Album

You have tons of photos from your (insert big monumental event here) just lying around. They're weighing on you, but you don't have time to get them scrapped. Have no fear! No, a scrapbooking superhero isn't going to come scrap for you. But you can create a mini album like Jennifer's. You can continue working on the "real" album at your own pace, but at least you have the memory captured.

5 *Getting Tech Savvy*

Now that I've gone digital, I've discovered all kinds of tech-related shortcuts to make my scrapbooking faster. It's true, though, that the computer doesn't always make everything easier, especially when you don't know what you're doing. There is a bit of a learning curve at first when you start making hybrid or digital pages. But once you figure a few things out, technology can save you tons of scrapbooking time and hassle!

Whether you are creating pages digitally or just adding a few digital touches here and there, the computer can be your greatest tool in the quest to save some minutes. Read on for some great ideas to shave your work time in half!

L'il 'Poser'

Ethan has always been a ham ball, but this surprised me.... I asked for a smile and i got a whole series of poses, most of which absolutely cracked me up. I loved that he wanted to be my little model! 9/07

Resize Photos Digitally

Back when I used film, one of my least favorite things to do was crop photos to get exactly the right sizes. Now, I almost always place photos on a 12" x 12" (30cm x 30cm) digital canvas. Once I've sized and positioned them, I print the entire block as one photo. In this case, I also added a frame and a title before printing.

The 4th of July always makes me so happy to live in a small town!

The celebration starts early with breakfast with our friends...

and we all head over a block to watch the best-ever July 4th parade!

They still throw lots of candy, so the kids are in heaven!

Days like this are chock-full of happy!

small town 4th!

Predetermine Journaling Space

Fifteen photos plus journaling on a one-page layout: Are you kidding? This layout could not have been simpler! Laying out the photos in an image-editing program helped me determine how long my journaling strips needed to be before I created the layout. Look for pockets of white space on a page where you can add your own journaling.

2006

Sophia's class had so much fun at their Christmas party.
The highlight had to be decorating these cookies... and of course, eating them!

I'm so glad I got to go and be a part of the fun!

christmas cookies

#1 Way to Get Tech Savvy

Learn how to use it!

If you don't know how to use image-editing software, work your printer or incorporate digital elements, then getting technical will waste more time than save it. Take some time, even spare moments, to read the printer manual or play around with the software's tools. Here's the key: Learn and practice before you ever use the technology for a layout. You may have to swap scrapping time for learning time at first, but it will save time in the end.

Keep Fonts Simple →

If you're like me, you've taken advantage of all the great free font sites online. You can download just about every kind of font. But if you're looking to move quickly, keep the font simple. For this layout, I relied on a tried-and-true clean font, Century Gothic, for both the title and journaling. I love the way it looks, and it was a no-brainer in getting this page finished.

why so scared?

It was the firecrackers. Aren't these things illegal or something?
Uncle Chad and Uncle Matt had a stash to fill the trunk of the car...
and they spent most of the fourth setting them off.
The girls were caught off guard several times... and it's pretty easy to see
how they felt about the whole thing.

Frame Photos Before Printing

Sometimes using your computer simply means adding a digital frame to
a photo before printing it. This eliminates the need for a photo mat,
allowing your picture to pop right off the page from the get-go. I knew
I wanted to use black as an accent color on this layout, so the black
frame helped reinforce my color scheme and make the picture stand out.

Is there anything better than a hot summer afternoon spent outside in the sun, running in the sprinkler with all your cousins and cooling off with your favorite kind of popsicle? We made it a point to spend lots of these kinds of days this summer, and I am so glad we did. Knowing we only have a couple of months with no school made it that much more important because I just miss you so much during the year. These are the kinds of tiny memories I'm going to hold onto, Sophia. That face, those crazy long eyelashes, the giggles at getting soaking wet. I just love these long summer days with you. 8/07

summer magic

"Sew" with Digital Stitches

I love the way machine stitches look on a layout, but it can be time-consuming and it takes more skill than I've got! If you can relate, that's OK, because now we can get the same look on our lay-outs digitally ... and in a lot less time! Just open up the stitch file and drag the stitching onto your page to instantly create what looks like a machine-stitched border. Sew easy!

Say hello to Max. Can you see him? He's up there on the top right side of the bug box. He's a grasshopper and was unfortunate enough to find himself inside our screen door yesterday. Liam caught him and immediately named him Max. The next step was, of course, to find out what Max would like to eat. Liam suggested we look it up on the internet (kids have it so easy these days!!). We found that depending on the species, grasshoppers like plants and sometimes grass. Because we didn't know what specie he was (and I wasn't getting close enough to find out), Liam found both a plant and grass and a flower to for good measure. Liam and Ashlyn made plans to watch Max grow to be bigger than the cage and at that point they would let him go because he would be "raised". They would then find another grasshopper and start all over again. I then asked how they knew that he wasn't already full grown. I was looked at as if I had two heads and they went back to their scheming and plans for a "grasshopper raising business". Eventually I broke the news that we would probably have to let Max go today in order for him to survive. I explained that grasshoppers needed their freedom and that he probably didn't like to be cooped up. Liam suggested we find a cage as big as the backyard so that Max would have plenty of room to jump and hop! Ah...the imagination of a child. In the end, we all agreed to let Max go on to a better life. It was good knowing you Max.

06.07

MEET

max

Artwork by Greta Hammond

Busy Scrapper

Greta Hammond
stays digitally organized

For me, the most time-consuming aspect of scrapbooking is dealing with the magnitude of photos. I've found that using my computer to organize my photos as well as plan out pages has saved me a lot of time. I download my photos frequently and create folders by date and then by activity. When I actually go to print photos for my pages, I create a canvas in Photoshop and lay out my page with the photos before printing. I love being organized, and having materials on my computer keeps it all at my fingertips!

Take Advantage of Blogs

Blogs are a wildly popular and wonderful online format for a journal. The best thing is, they enable you to keep an extensive archive, complete with dated entries that tell exactly what you were thinking and when. For this layout, Greta converted a blog entry into a scrapbook page in a cinch because the journaling was already accompanying the photos. What a great timesaver!

Create a Custom Background

Artwork by Jennifer Pebbles

For this hybrid layout, Jennifer was able to create her own background using her computer. She printed the design on a sheet of textured cardstock and added the other elements. It was a quick way to get a great decorative look, saving her the time of searching for the perfect products to go along with her photos.

Who says friends have to be the same age? Miss Stephanie is more than just a babysitter or a secretary or a girl we know from church. She is one of those people who has the innate ability to understand kids and somehow, it is so clear she really thinks of them as her little friends. We all feel so lucky to have her in our lives, but I think it's our kids who are getting the most out of it!

a friend is someone who touches your heart.

Copy Digital Elements →

A cluster of digital elements is a simple way to give your page some interest in no time. Simply copy one element as I did with these flowers, change up the size and create a group alongside a photograph. It's quick, but punchy—just what this page needed!

couldn't be happier

When I look at this picture, it reminds me of these family events where we get to go to my parents house and get together with my brother and sister and their families. This picture is the epitome of happiness - exactly how I feel when I'm there. I love the way we can all just relax together and hang out without feeling awkward or strange. It's so comfortable, and catching up with these guys and their kids is the best possible way to spend a holiday. July 4th at Mom and Dad's will forever be one of my very favorite memories. July 4th, 2007

➤ Go Happily Hybrid

This layout started as a digital page, and I thought it would end up that way, too. But when I printed out my title, journaling and photo frame, I saw it would make a great start to a traditional layout. After I printed the page, I trimmed off the bottom and built a square layout around it. It came together quickly because my main features were done on the computer.

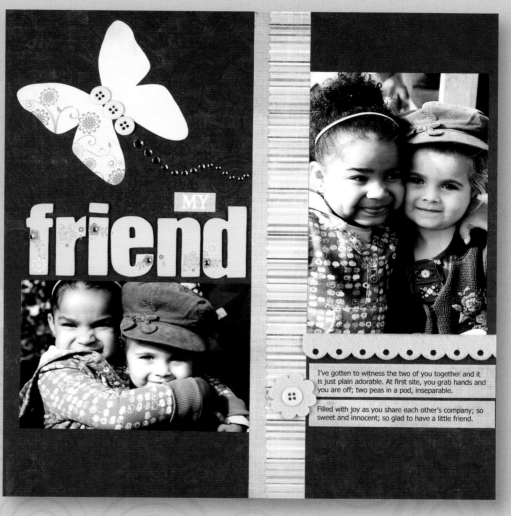

Digitally Sketch Your Layouts

Using sketches is a great way to ensure quick assembly of a page. You can make your own "sketches" using an image-editing program like Photoshop Elements as Greta has done here. Armed with a good idea of where she wanted to place her photos and her title, Greta was able to put this layout together in just minutes.

Artwork by Greta Hammond

Artwork by Jennifer Pebbles

Enlarge a Background Photo

The beauty of digital photography is that you can do whatever you want with it. An uncluttered photo makes a stunning background for a layout like Jennifer's. Just enlarge a digital photo and print! And take this design cue from Jennifer: Limit the colors in the background picture to allow a focal point photo to really shine with its bright hues.

Kick-Start Challenge

Kick it up a digital notch! Challenge your creative self to go a step further in using technology.

If the extent of your digital scrapbooking is printing out photos, try printing out journaling as well. If you already make digital sketches or you lay out your photos using image-editing software, try making an entirely digital page.

In the process of trying a new technique, you may discover new ways to increase your productivity.

Scrap a Digital Page

One night, I really wanted to scrapbook, but I didn't feel like dragging out all my supplies. The alternative? Do it all digitally. No photos to print or glue to get out. With digital, all you have to drag is your mouse. You get all the same supplies, like paper, alphas and embellishments, but at the end of the day there's no mess to clean up.

so much fun at navy pier

summer '06

In the middle of a really, bad day I caught this.
And suddenly the day didn't seem so bad anymore.

Don't Fuss with Color

The easiest way to learn digital scrapbooking is to keep it simple. I decided not to fuss over this page, so I incorporated the absence of color. Sometimes, there's no need to spend time picking out patterns or colors. Just let a gorgeous photo stand on its own. Not cluttering your digital toolbox allows you to focus on the basics and still end up with a stunning layout.

"But I'm not good with computers!" Yeah, I know. I've been there. Photoshop Elements was on my computer for years before I opened it. But once I did, I spent a little time reading up on various tutorials and finally got more comfortable with the program. Now I rarely scrap without it. Invest in a simple image-editing program and use it for sketches, resizing photos and, when you're comfortable, tackling digital and hybrid layouts. You'll never turn back!

Stick to Digital Basics

Digital doesn't always mean fast. There are just as many products and complicated techniques as with paper scrapping. Guess what? You don't have to use tons of embellishments to create your pages. There's something about the simplicity of a simple background and just a few details that is so attractive. Plus, adding drop shadows and some brushstrokes can be done in less than a minute flat.

Make Mini Album Templates

I love mini books. They're cute and fun, and I love the sense of accomplishment I get when I finish. In order to make mini book-making simpler, I turn to the computer. I create a digital template or two, plug in my information and print. Once it's printed, you can embellish a mini album with a few traditional scrapbooking supplies and call it a day.

Create Monthly Templates

Templates aren't reserved for mini albums. Use them to create a year's worth of layouts. At the beginning of the year, create a digital page and use that as a template for 11 more monthly pages. Save all 12 pages so they're ready to go at the end of each month—just insert photos and you're done! The great thing about digital is that you can e-mail the pages to family and friends.

6 Finding Inspiration

Lack of inspiration can play a big role in time-consuming scrapping. After all, if you're stuck, you're stuck—it's hard to move forward and get things done. There's no substitute for great inspiration. It's too bad, really, that you can't fake it. I'd love an artificially sweetened version of inspiration, but it just doesn't exist. Instead, you have to constantly keep your creative gas tank full of fuel and be ready to attack your pages at any moment. So this chapter gives you several ideas on how to get—and stay—inspired, making that next layout a quick and easy reality instead of a distant dream.

The other day I overheard a conversation between you, your friend Courtney Rose and a boy that you had met at the park. The new boy started talking about people of different races. After a little while when Courtney talked about her race and color I could tell from what you said that you had not really noticed that she was "different" than you. Later, I asked you if you had ever wondered why her skin color was different than yours. You said, "Not really. I thought she was almost the same as me except she's a girl." Does it matter that she is different than you? "No. Just as long as she doesn't want me to play a lot of girl stuff, 'cause I really don't like some of that."

growing up

Colorblind

What color are SouLS? she said and I said, COLOR isn't that much of an issue when you're talking SOULS." Brian Andreas

09072007

Artwork by Linda Albrecht

Keep an Inspiration Notebook

Keep track of your inspiration with a notebook. Even a basic spiral one is just right for recording page ideas, quotes, colors and patterns you like. Like Linda—who grabbed this Brian Andreas quote from her notebook—when your creativity needs a little coaxing, you'll have a wealth of ideas to choose from!

Pick up Pieces From Others

Maybe you don't want to actually scraplift another person's layout, but you can certainly allow other layouts to inspire your own creations. Nic's use of transparencies in "Beautiful A" (on page 109) inspired me to create this layout. I followed a similar design, stacking most of my embellishments to the lower left of my photo and including a journaling strip. While I owe the idea to Nic, the end result is very much my own.

Let Family Inspire You

Family members are the inspiration for so much that we do in life, and they make great inspiration for layouts, too. Nic's layout here is a testament to that fact. If you're feeling burned out scrapping holidays and events, step back and just think about someone you love. What comes to mind? What do you love about them? What quirks do they have? How are you similar? Then find a photo and get to work!

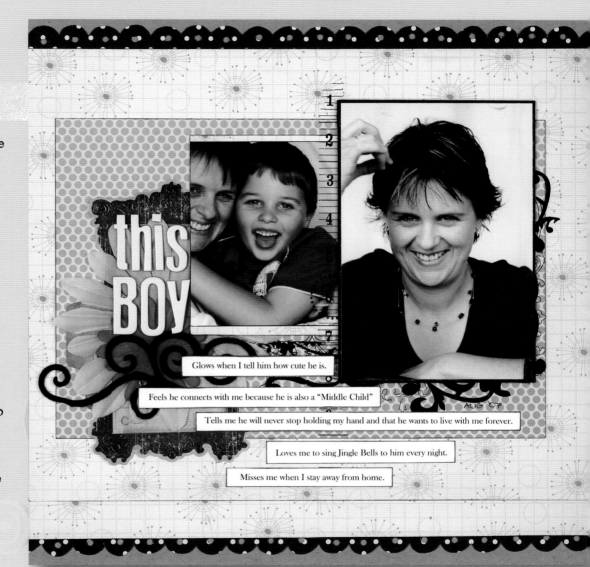

this BOY

Glows when I tell him how cute he is.

Feels he connects with me because he is also a "Middle Child"

Tells me he will never stop holding my hand and that he wants to live with me forever.

Loves me to sing Jingle Bells to him every night.

Misses me when I stay away from home.

AUG '07

Artwork by Nic Howard

Nic Howard
reuses great ideas

I love the feeling of accomplishment when something goes right—like a color combination that worked so well or the perfect set of embellishments. One of my favorite ways to save time is to use ideas I love on more than one layout. Sometimes I reuse my layout designs. I'll try a mirror image, flip it, spin it or turn it around for variations. It's surprising how different layouts can look, even when they are repeating the elements already used. Using what I've got saves time planning and making decisions.

Beautiful A

I am looking forward to the coming year.

It will be your last year before school.

You will be old enough to do things with me,

Yet young enough to still be my little friend.

November 2007.

Artwork by Nic Howard

Use Designs Again

There's nothing that says you can't be inspired by yourself. Got a great layout design? Use it again! You can create several different-looking layouts using the same basic design! Take Nic's page here: Although the design in "Beautiful A" was inspired by "This Boy" (on the previous page), the two pages don't look like twins.

#1 Way to Get Inspired

Look for inspiration!

You can't get inspired without inspiration. Constantly challenge yourself to see things through new eyes. From book covers to TV commercials to billboards to clothing, inspiration is everywhere if you are willing to look for it! A shift in your thinking can open up a whole new world of possibilities, so what are you waiting for?

Artwork by Heather Burch

Borrow from Books

The next time you're looking for some playful inspiration, turn to your favorite children's book. A *Charlie and Lola* book Heather had on hand inspired her layout here. With all the bright colors and fun designs in children's books, you've got a wealth of inspiration right at your fingertips!

I pray you two are the best of friends.
ethan loving newborn Sam 11/07

my brother

Flip Through Catalogs

My husband said to me recently, "You have more magazines than anyone I know," to which I replied, "Have you been to my mom's house?" We had a little debate about keeping every bit of printed materials, and I think I won. This layout is the result of inspiration that struck while perusing a Pottery Barn catalog. The color combination of black and light blue inspired me and easily transferred to this layout.

Play with Product

Sometimes you need to jumpstart your creativity. For Virginia, creating a tag, flower or small embellishment is often the push she needs. When she started this layout, she says she had no mojo. A few minutes of playing with a stamp set, some ink, thick plastic and a heat gun, and an idea was born. Stuck for inspiration? Start with a little bit of play!

Artwork by Virginia Williams

it's always a little embarrassing posing like this with Carrie & Lindsey every family function, but... what a cool record of us over the years! Worth a bit of embarrassment, I'd say! 2006

FAMILY IS THE LAST AND
GREATEST DISCOVERY.
IT IS OUR LAST MIRACLE.

Kitchen photo

other things may change us, but we start and end with family - anthony brandt

Start with Patterns

I assume your paper collection is mostly patterns you bought
yourself. If you purchased it, odds are there was something about
it you loved. This sheet of patterned paper was the inspiration here;
I wanted to find a photo to use with it. It might be backwards, but
it's easier to scrapbook when you're inspired, and the products at
your fingertips are an excellent source of inspiration!

Peruse a Thesaurus

Next time you only sort of know what you want to say, turn to a thesaurus for inspiration! Initially, Virginia wanted a title that said how adorable her baby boy is. But adorable wasn't cutting it. Enter, the thesaurus. After perusing the choices, she saw the word "cute," which reminded her of a phrase she's often repeating. And just like that, a title was born!

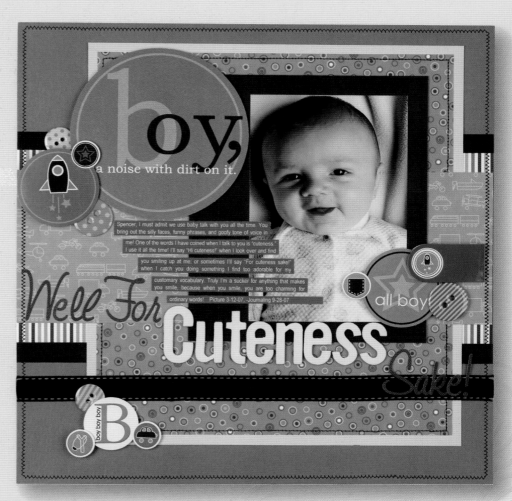

Artwork by Virginia Williams

Keep a Quote Book

Quotes are great for kick-starting creativity and providing topics for layouts. But it's easy to lose or forget those you hear, leaving you stumped for words. Consider scrapping a notebook like Linda's specifically for those gems that are sure to inspire future layouts!

Timesaving Tools

Inspiration Station

While it may not seem like an essential "tool," a space set aside for displaying inspiration—like a bulletin board of ideas or a shelf lined with books—actually can function that way. Surrounding yourself with images you love can't help but inspire you, and ultimately that will make your scrapping fast. Plus, you'll never lose your sources of inspiration when they're right in front of you!

Artwork by Linda Albrecht

Pull From Photos

One of the most obvious ways to gain inspiration is to look to the photos you are scrapping, pulling color and pattern directly from them. For this page about our trip to Nantucket, the photo of the sign inspired me. The colors were so indicative of the island itself, so I allowed myself to go with that, and the rest of the page was a breeze!

Impressions of Nantucket:
I felt like I was stepping onto a movie set, to be honest. It's only in movies I've seen people travel by bicycle complete with a basket of flowers in the front. The cobblestone streets, the smell of the ocean. The buildings were old and brick and beautiful, and I still cannot get the picture of this island out of my head. As we strolled down the brick sidewalks, I imagined myself living here. I imagined the feeling of joy the people on this island must have just to be surrounded by water and beauty and quaint charm. This island left such an impression on me, and I hope one day Adam and I will go back. I would love to explore more of this place - this delightful little island I am so glad to have visited... if only for a day.

It is hard to believe but *Green Eggs and Ham* really only has 50 words in it! I figured this fact made it a perfect book to start teaching you boys to read. Ty, so far you know more of the words than Blake—and you are getting good at yelling out all the words you know; yet both of you are quickly picking up on the patterns and repetitions of the story. Reading this book with you boys reminds me of learning to read through *Hop on Pop* with my parents; I had it memorized just as you two are memorizing this book! —Fall '07

Artwork by Virginia Williams

Check Your Desk

After creating a card, Virginia found her desk covered with scraps. Rather than tuck them away, she dove in and came up with this layout. Says Virginia, "The layout was fast and easy because all my supplies were right at my fingertips." Next time you're looking for quick inspiration, check what's right on your desk.

It's more than just the short legs that I got from you. I'd say we're alike in a lot of different ways. We're both incredibly stubborn. We both have great sense of direction. Thanks to you, I've got a healthy dose of common sense. I think I inherited your work ethic... it's a pretty good list of traits you've passed down.

I feel lucky to be able to say I'm a lot like you.

a lot like you.

Look Past the Obvious

I took this picture at my niece's birthday party. Later, when I intended to do a layout about the party, I stumbled upon this picture. Looking at it, I found an entirely different story—a page I'd been wanting to create about my similarities to my dad. Look past the obvious for inspiration. Sometimes the unintended will emerge and bring a new page to life.

Challenge Yourself

Sometimes a challenge is what you need for inspiration and breaking yourself out of a rut. For this layout, I asked Greta to pull out just a few products to use. Once she gathered the stash, she couldn't add to it; she had to use what was there. Fired up by meeting a challenge, Greta was able to create quickly and with beautiful results!

The three of you are very fortunate to have such a caring and involved Grandma. She would say that she is lucky to have you but I would say that you are the lucky ones.

Artwork by Greta Hammond

Supply Lists

Page 20 Fall Fun
Cardstock; patterned paper (American Crafts); chipboard letters (Heidi Swapp); chipboard leaf (BasicGrey); Misc: Times New Roman font

Page 21 Christmas '07
Cardstock; flower, patterned paper, stamp (Scarlet Lime); brad, letter stickers (Making Memories); ink (Ranger); pen (American Crafts)

Page 22 I Heart You
Patterned paper (My Mind's Eye); letter stickers (American Crafts); chipboard heart (Pressed Petals); ink (Ranger); Misc: buttons, floss, pen

Page 23 Laugh
Patterned paper (Scenic Route); chipboard letters (Heidi Swapp); rub-on (Chatterbox); pen (American Crafts)

Page 24 Animated
Cardstock (Prism); chipboard stickers, patterned paper (Creative Imaginations); chipboard letters (Heidi Swapp); brads (Making Memories); flowers (American Crafts); Misc: pen

Page 25 I Wish
Die-cut flowers, patterned paper (Fancy Pants); chipboard letters (Heidi Swapp); button (Autumn Leaves); Misc: Century Gothic font, floss

Page 26 Little Swimmer
Brads, flowers, letter stickers, patterned paper (Making Memories); ink (Ranger); pen (EK Success)

Page 27 Drafted
Cardstock; number cardstock (KI Memories); patterned paper (EK Success, Scenic Route); chipboard letters (BasicGrey); rub-ons (Heidi Swapp); Misc: ink, pen

Page 28 Summer
Cardstock (Prism); chipboard letters (American Crafts); brads, flowers (Queen & Co.); pen (American Crafts)

Page 29 Thankful
Cardstock (Prism); buttons, patterned paper (Making Memories); chipboard letters (American Crafts); chipboard flourish (Rusty Pickle); Misc: Century Gothic font, floss, paint

Page 30 Baptism Day
Patterned paper (BasicGrey); die-cut paper, rub-ons, ticket stub (Jenni Bowlin); letter stickers, stamp (Poppy Ink); brads, chipboard buttons, trim (Making Memories); crochet flower (Imaginisce); buttons (BasicGrey, Buttons Galore); photo turns (BasicGrey); chipboard crown (Me & My Big Ideas); date sticker (EK Success)

Page 31 Tree Climber
Patterned paper (BasicGrey, My Mind's Eye, Rusty Pickle, Scenic Route); transparency (Rusty Pickle); title letters (American Crafts, Making Memories); number stickers (Autumn Leaves); brads (Making Memories); Misc: Euphorigenic font, ink

Page 32 Make a Wish
Cardstock; brads, die-cut shapes, patterned paper, sticker accents (Pebbles); chipboard letters (Heidi Swapp); Misc: SP Toby Type font, adhesive foam, ink, pen

Page 33 Today
Cardstock (Prism); die-cut stickers, patterned paper (Melissa Frances); chipboard letters (Imagination Project); buttons (Autumn Leaves)

Page 34 Laughter
Cardstock; brads, letter stickers, patterned paper (Chatterbox); Misc: Times New Roman font, pen

Page 35 Home
Cardstock; letter stickers, patterned paper (Chatterbox); buttons (Autumn Leaves); Misc: floss, pen

Page 36 Love My Boy
Cardstock (Bazzill, Prism); letter stickers (Doodlebug); brads (Queen & Co.); ink (Ranger); Misc: pen

Page 37 Hopscotch
Cardstock; patterned paper (Autumn Leaves, Rhonna Designs); chipboard letters (Autumn Leaves); stamps (7gypsies, Hero Arts); transparency border (Rhonna Designs); Misc: Cheryl font, buttons, flowers, gems, ink

Page 38 Bonding
Cardstock (Prism); patterned paper (Daisy D's, Me & My Big Ideas); letter stickers (SEI); die-cut shapes (Daisy D's); button (Autumn Leaves); rickrack (Melissa Frances)

Page 39 Solid
Cardstock (Prism); die-cut shapes, patterned paper (October Afternoon); letter stickers (American Crafts); ink (Ranger); Misc: Arial font, floss

Page 40 Feeling Shy
Cardstock (Prism); patterned paper, photo corners (Making Memories); die-cut shapes (Provo Craft); Misc: Batik Regular font

Page 41 Meeting Boss
Cardstock; patterned paper (Scarlet Lime); scalloped cardstock (Creative Imaginations); letter stickers, paper frills, rub-on stitches (Doodlebug); button (Autumn Leaves); pen (EK Success); Misc: Abadi MT Condensed font

Page 44 Pumpkin Love
Cardstock; buttons, die-cut shapes, patterned paper (BasicGrey); Misc: vintage book page

Page 45 At First Sight
Cardstock (Prism); patterned paper, trim (Scarlet Lime); scalloped cardstock (Creative Imaginations); chipboard letters (American Crafts); word sticker (Me & My Big Ideas); journaling stamps (7gypsies); pen (American Crafts)

Page 46 Homework
Cardstock (Prism); cardstock stickers, patterned paper (Rusty Pickle); chipboard letters (American Crafts); ink (Ranger); Misc: adhesive foam, pen

Page 47 Unlikely Pair
Patterned paper (BasicGrey, KI Memories, Paper+Cup, Tinkering Ink); letter stickers (Scenic Route); die-cut paper, scallop stickers (KI Memories); chipboard accents (Doodlebug, Scenic Route); rub-ons (BasicGrey); Misc: glitter

Page 48 Cute
Cardstock; die-cut shapes, patterned paper, ribbon, stickers (Pebbles); Misc: Century Gothic font

Page 49 Grammy
Kraft paper; patterned paper, trim (Scarlet Lime); chipboard letters (American Crafts); circle, journaling and scallop stickers (Creative Imaginations); ink (Ranger)

Page 50 But I Wanted to Win
Cardstock (Prism); patterned paper (American Crafts); letter stickers (Doodlebug); chipboard arrows (Rusty Pickle); buttons (Autumn Leaves); Misc: floss

Page 51 Spiderman
Patterned paper (EK Success); letter stickers (American Crafts, Doodlebug, KI Memories, Making Memories); sticker accents (Sandylion); Misc: Abadi MT Condensed font

Page 52 Home on Christmas
Cardstock (Prism); patterned paper, photo corner, stickers, trim (Melissa Frances); definition stickers (Making Memories); letter stickers (Mustard Moon); button (Autumn Leaves); ink (Ranger)

Page 53 Laughter
Patterned paper (BasicGrey, Mustard Moon); letter stickers (Mustard Moon); number sticker (Daisy D's); buttons (Autumn Leaves); sequins (Westrim); Misc: 1942 Report, Adler, Bliss and Euphorigenic fonts, circle punch, ink, paint

Page 54 Sam Loves Grammy
Cardstock (Prism); patterned paper (Chatterbox, EK Success, SEI); chipboard letters, letter stickers (American Crafts); chipboard heart (Rusty Pickle); button (Autumn Leaves); ribbon (Chatterbox); pen (Sakura)

Page 55 October
Cardstock; patterned paper (Making Memories, Creative Imaginations); letter stickers (American Crafts, Making Memories); chipboard buttons, ribbon (KI Memories); sticker accents (Making Memories)

Page 56 Daddy Love
Cardstock; chipboard letters (Heidi Swapp); chipboard heart (Pressed Petals); border stickers (Imagination Project); Misc: Arial font, floss

Page 57 On Top of the World
Cardstock; patterned paper (Scenic Route); letter stickers (Imagination Project, Scenic Route); button (Autumn Leaves); felt butterfly (Provo Craft); Misc: Batik Regular font, chipboard letters, paint

Page 58 Pirate Princess
Cardstock (Prism); cardstock stickers, patterned paper (Rusty Pickle); trim (Scarlet Lime)

Page 59 Such a Big Imagination
Cardstock (Prism); chipboard stars, patterned paper (Rusty Pickle); glitter (Ranger); jewels (Doodlebug); Misc: lace

Page 60 Smile
Cardstock; lace cardstock, ribbon, sticker tab (KI Memories); patterned paper (KI Memories, Scenic Route); letter stickers (American Crafts); chipboard heart (Heidi Swapp); tag (Martha Stewart); photo turn (7gypsies); brad (Making Memories); Misc: Century Gothic

Page 61 Big Fun
Cardstock (Prism); chipboard letters (BasicGrey); brads, buttons, felt, flowers, sequins (Queen & Co.); jewels, letter stickers, paper frills (Doodlebug); ribbon, paint (Pebbles)

Page 62 Brilliantly Simple
Chipboard accents, die-cut shapes, letter stickers, patterned paper (BasicGrey); rickrack (Rusty Pickle); ink (Ranger); pen (EK Success)

Page 63 Thanks Card
Cardstock (Prism); chipboard and die-cut shapes, letter stickers (BasicGrey); rickrack (Rusty Pickle); ink (Ranger)

Page 64 Fall Frolic
Cardstock; patterned paper (Scenic Route); letter stickers (American Crafts, Doodlebug); chipboard frames (EK Success); Misc: ink, pen

Page 65 Onward and Upward
Chipboard letters and shape, die-cut shapes, letter stickers, patterned paper, rub-ons (Scenic Route); Misc: 2 Peas Hot Chocolate font, ink

Page 66 Volcano Falls
Cardstock (Prism); transparency (Hambly); patterned paper (KI Memories); paper frills (Doodlebug); chipboard phrase (Scenic Route); ribbon (Pebbles)

Page 67 Budding Artist
Cardstock; patterned paper (Chatterbox); die-cut letters (QuicKutz); buttons (Autumn Leaves); Misc: Arial font, floss, ink

Page 68 A Home Run? Well, Almost
Cardstock; patterned paper (American Crafts); letter stickers (Arctic Frog); metal-rimmed tags (Making Memories); Misc: adhesive foam

Page 69 Soccer '07
Cardstock; patterned paper (CherryArte); letter stickers (Heidi Swapp); number stickers (Doodlebug); chipboard stars (Li'l Davis); dimensional glaze (JudiKins); Misc: ink, pen, staples

Page 72 School Days
Cardstock; patterned paper (Scenic Route); letter stickers (KI Memories); chipboard arrows (Rusty Pickle); ribbon (Chatterbox); Misc: Tahoma font, paint

Page 73 Check Me Out
Cardstock (Prism); letter stickers, patterned paper (American Crafts); brads, flowers, photo turns (Queen & Co.); Misc: Century Gothic font

Page 74 Sass
Cardstock; flowers, letter stickers, patterned paper, photo corners, ribbon (Chatterbox); ink (Ranger); Misc: Century Gothic font, floss, staples

Page 75 Thanks
Felt stickers, patterned paper (Tinkering Ink); felt flowers (Queen & Co.); notecard (Target)

Page 76 Changed
Photos by Christy Miller
Cardboard; patterned paper, ribbon (unknown); letter stickers (American Crafts); word stickers (Making Memories); button (Autumn Leaves); trim (Scarlet Lime); ink (Ranger); pen (EK Success)

Page 77 Return the Favor
Cardstock, chipboard flower, die-cut shapes, letter stickers, patterned paper (BasicGrey); buttons (Autumn Leaves); Misc: Abadi MT Condensed font, floss

Page 78 Complete
Cardstock (Prism); journaling tag, patterned paper, rub-ons (October Afternoon); letter stickers (Mustard Moon); buttons (Autumn Leaves); chipboard arrows (Rusty Pickle); paint (Pebbles)

Page 79 When You Grow Up
Patterned paper (BasicGrey, Creative Imaginations, EK Success); chipboard accents (Making Memories); letter stickers (Autumn Leaves, BasicGrey); ribbon (Offray); rub-ons (American Crafts, Creative Imaginations, Doodlebug, Making Memories); brads, buttons (Autumn Leaves, Making Memories, vintage); bracket, photo turns (Rusty Pickle); Misc: ink, paint

Page 80 Pucker Up
Cardstock (Prism); patterned paper (Deja Views); chipboard letters (American Crafts); buttons (Autumn Leaves); chipboard accent (Rusty Pickle); brad, flower, word stickers (Making Memories); glitter, ink (Ranger); Misc: Courier New font, floss

Page 80 True Friend
Cardstock; cardstock stickers, crochet flower, patterned paper, photo corners (Anna Griffin); letter stickers (American Crafts); ink (Ranger); Misc: Century Gothic font

Page 81 Favorite Friend
Cardstock sticker, crochet flower, patterned paper (Anna Griffin); word stickers (Making Memories); ink (Ranger)

Page 82 Beautiful
Cardstock (Prism); patterned paper (American Crafts); letter stickers (Mustard Moon); chipboard accents (BasicGrey); buttons (Autumn Leaves)

Page 83 Soup
Cardstock; patterned paper (KI Memories); brads, chipboard letters, word sticker (Making Memories); ribbon (Martha Stewart); Misc: ink

Page 84 Indigo Girls
Cardstock; chipboard letter (Li'l Davis); stamps (PSX); Misc: ink, pen, ribbon, staples

Page 85 Wedding Album
Die-cut chipboard (Scenic Route); patterned paper (Making Memories); digital patterned paper (Two Peas in a Bucket); tag (BasicGrey); acrylic letter, chipboard letters (Heidi Swapp); ribbon (KI Memories)

Page 88 L'il 'Poser'
Cardstock (Prism); buttons, felt (Queen & Co.); digital photo frame (Designer Digitals); ink (Ranger); Misc: Coperniq font, pen

Page 89 Small Town 4th
Cardstock (Prism); letter stickers (American Crafts); felt stars (Queen & Co.); Misc: Century Gothic font

Page 90 Christmas Cookies
Digital patterned paper and stitches (Shabby Princess); curled edge frame by Katie Pertiet (Designer Digitals); Misc: Century Gothic font

Page 91 Why So Scared?
Cardstock (Prism); patterned paper (7gypsies, EK Success); letter stickers (American Crafts); paper frills, rhinestones (Doodlebug); chipboard flower (BasicGrey); paint (Pebbles); Misc: Arial font

Page 92 Summer Magic
Digital notepaper, patterned paper and staple by Leah Riordan (Oscraps); inked edge by Gina Cabrera (Digital Design Essentials); stitches (Shabby Princess); Misc: Century Gothic font

Page 93 Meet Max
Chipboard letters, die-cut shapes, patterned paper, rub-ons (Fancy Pants); letter stickers (EK Success); button (Autumn Leaves); ink (Ranger); Misc: Times New Roman font, paint

Page 94 New Home
Cardstock; digital damask overlay (Two Peas in a Bucket); brads, clip (Making Memories); word stickers (Making Memories, Scrapworks); tickets (Jenni Bowlin); stamps (Bunch Of Fun); Misc: Century Gothic font, ink

Page 95 A Friend
Digital patterned paper by Heather Melzer (Heather Ann Designs); Misc: Eight Track and Gill Sans fonts

Page 96 Couldn't Be Happier
Cardstock (Prism); patterned paper (Scarlet Lime); buttons (Autumn Leaves); ribbon (Pebbles); Misc: Century Gothic

Page 97 My Friend
Chipboard letters, die-cut shapes, felt trim, patterned paper, rub-ons (Fancy Pants); Misc: buttons, paint, rhinestones

Page 98 Public Market
Photo by Maria Grace Abuzman
Cardstock; word stickers (Making Memories); labels (Autumn Leaves, Jenni Bowlin); Misc: glitter

Page 99 Navy Pier
Digital patterned paper by Sande Krieger (Two Peas in a Bucket); Misc: Cry Kitty font

Page 100 Make My Day
Digital journaling stamp (Designer Digitals); stitches (Shabby Princess); Misc: Century Gothic and Susie's Hand fonts, digital brush

Page 101 Accidental Bangs
Digital brush by Rhonna Farrer (Two Peas in a Bucket); Misc: AL Sandra and Century Gothic fonts

Page 102 Little Book of Bible Verses
Digital patterned paper (Shabby Princess); tabs (Scrapworks); flowers (American Crafts, Target); flower charm (Around The Block); brads, button, sequins, swirl (Queen & Co.); buttons (Autumn Leaves); digital brush by Rhonna Farrer (Two Peas in a Bucket); Misc: Willing Race font, ribbon

Page 103 Christmas '06
Digital snowflakes by Rhonna Farrer (Two Peas in a Bucket); inked edge by Gina Cabrera (Digital Design Essentials); Misc: Gigi font

Page 106 Colorblind
Patterned paper (BasicGrey, EK Success, My Mind's Eye, Scenic Route); acrylic letters, buttons, clip (Making Memories); chipboard accents, lace (Rusty Pickle); rub-ons (Heidi Grace); rhinestones (Crafts, Etc.); sequins (Westrim); Misc: Adler font, floss, ink, thread, transparency

Page 107 Treat
Cardstock (Prism); scalloped cardstock (Creative Imaginations); patterned paper (My Mind's Eye); chipboard letters (Making Memories); transparency (Hambly); stamps (KI Memories); felt butterfly (Tattered Tags); paint (Pebbles); ink (Ranger); pen (American Crafts)

Page 108 This Boy
Cardstock; patterned paper (Scenic Route); chipboard letters, flowers (Heidi Swapp); felt swirls (Queen & Co.); rub-ons (BasicGrey, Daisy D's, Fontwerks); Misc: Trebuchet MS font

Page 109 Beautiful A
Cardstock; chipboard and sticker accents, patterned paper (Creative Imaginations); transparency (Rusty Pickle); stamps (Gelatins); Misc: My Own Topher font, ink

Page 110 You Are My Favorite and My Best
Patterned paper (Rusty Pickle); letter stickers (American Crafts, Scenic Route); rub-ons (Hambly); labels (Scenic Route); crochet flower (My Mind's Eye); flowers (7gypsies); vellum file folder (Maya Road); date sticker (EK Success); Misc: vintage book pages, buttons and ticket

Page 111 My Brother
Cardstock; patterned paper (Prima); brads, letter stickers (Chatterbox); chipboard shapes (Making Memories); grommets (Scrapworks); buttons (Autumn Leaves); pen (Sakura)

Page 112 Sweet Ride
Cardstock; patterned paper (Mustard Moon); stamps (Gelatins); embossing powder (Ranger); brads (Queen & Co.); Misc: acrylic sheet, adhesive, letter stickers

Page 113 Kitchen
Cardstock (Prism); patterned paper (Prism, Sassafras Lass); letter stickers (Making Memories); flowers (K&Co.); quote stickers (Scenic Route); scalloped edge (Melissa Frances)

Page 114 Well, for Cuteness Sake
Cardstock; cardstock accents, patterned paper, ribbon, stickers (Pebbles); buttons (Making Memories); chipboard letters, letter stickers (BasicGrey)

Page 115 Quote Book
Notebook (Target); patterned paper, resin pieces, rub-ons (Melissa Frances); lace and trims (BasicGrey, Melissa Frances, Wrights); acrylic letters, clip (Making Memories); flower clip, tags (Creative Imaginations); button, string (Martha Stewart)

Page 116 Nantucket
Cardstock; patterned paper, rivets (Chatterbox); Misc: Century Gothic font

Page 117 Only 50 Words
Cardstock; patterned paper, themed accents (EK Success); brads, letter stickers (American Crafts)

Page 118 A Lot Like You
Cardstock (Prism); letter stickers, paint, patterned paper, ribbon (Pebbles); chipboard stars (BasicGrey); Misc: Century Gothic font

Page 119 Lucky Ones
Cardstock; patterned paper, ribbon (Rusty Pickle); chipboard letters (BasicGrey); rub-ons (Creative Imaginations); Misc: buttons, lace

Source Guide

The following companies manufacture products featured in this book. Please check your local retailers to find these materials, or go to a company's Web site for the latest product. In addition, we have made every attempt to properly credit the items mentioned in this book. We apologize to any company that we have listed incorrectly, and we would appreciate hearing from you. Companies with an asterisk (*) generously donated product toward the creation of the artwork in this book.

1001 Fonts
www.1001fonts.com

7gypsies
(877) 749-7797
www.sevengypsies.com

American Crafts*
(801) 226-0747
www.americancrafts.com

Anna Griffin, Inc.*
(888) 817-8170
www.annagriffin.com

Arctic Frog
www.arcticfrog.com

Around The Block
(801) 593-1946
www.aroundtheblockproducts.com

Autumn Leaves
(800) 588-6707
www.autumnleaves.com

BasicGrey*
(801) 544-1116
www.basicgrey.com

Bazzill Basics Paper
(480) 558-8557
www.bazzillbasics.com

Berwick Offray, LLC
(800) 237-9425
www.offray.com

Bunch Of Fun
www.bunchoffun.com

Buttons Galore & More
(856) 753-6700
www.buttonsgaloreandmore.com

Chatterbox, Inc.
(208) 461-5077
www.chatterboxinc.com

CherryArte
(212) 465-3495
www.cherryarte.com

Crafts, Etc. Ltd.
(800) 888-0321 x 1275
www.craftsetc.com

Creative Imaginations*
(800) 942-6487
www.cigift.com

Daisy D's Paper Company
(888) 601-8955
www.daisydspaper.com

Dèjá Views/C-Thru Ruler*
(800) 243-0303
www.dejaviews.com

Designer Digitals
www.designerdigitals.com

Digital Design Essentials
www.digitaldesignessentials.com

Doodlebug Design Inc.*
(877) 800-9190
www.doodlebug.ws

EK Success, Ltd.*
www.eksuccess.com

Fancy Pants Designs, LLC
(801) 779-3212
www.fancypantsdesigns.com

Fontwerks
(604) 942-3105
www.fontwerks.com

Gelatins*
(800) 393-2151
www.gelatinstamps.com

Hambly Screenprints
(800) 707-0977
www.hamblyscreenprints.com

Heather Ann Designs
www.heatheranndesigns.com

Heidi Grace Designs, Inc.*
(866) 347-5277
www.heidigrace.com

Heidi Swapp/Advantus Corporatio
(904) 482-0092
www.heidiswapp.com

Hero Arts Rubber Stamps, Inc.
(800) 822-4376
www.heroarts.com

Imagination Project, Inc.
(888) 477-6532
www.imaginationproject.com

Imaginisce
(801) 908-8111
www.imaginisce.com

Inque Boutique*
www.goinque.com

Jenni Bowlin
www.jennibowlin.com

JudiKins
(310) 515-1115
www.judikins.com

K&Company
(888) 244-2083
www.kandcompany.com

KI Memories
(972) 243-5595
www.kimemories.com

Li'l Davis Designs
(480) 223-0080
www.lildavisdesigns.com

Making Memories*
(801) 294-0430
www.makingmemories.com

Martha Stewart Crafts
www.marthastewartcrafts.com

Maya Road, LLC
(877) 427-7764
www.mayaroad.com

Me & My Big Ideas*
(949) 583-2065
www.meandmybigideas.com

Melissa Frances/
Heart & Home, Inc.*
(888) 616-6166
www.melissafrances.com

Mustard Moon*
(763) 493-5157
www.mustardmoon.com

My Mind's Eye, Inc.*
(800) 665-5116
www.mymindseye.com

October Afternoon
www.octoberafternoon.com

Offray- see Berwick Offray, LLC

Oscraps
www.oscraps.com

Paper + Cup Designs
(718) 852-1296
www.papercupdesign.com

Pebbles Inc.*
(801) 235-1520
www.pebblesink.com

Poppy Ink
www.poppyink.com

Pressed Petals
(801) 224-6766
www.pressedpetals.com

Prima Marketing, Inc.
(909) 627-5532
www.primamarketinginc.com

Prism Papers*
(866) 902-1002
www.prismpapers.com

Provo Craft
(800) 937-7686
www.provocraft.com

PSX Design
www.sierra-enterprises.com
/psxmain.html

Queen & Co.
(858) 613-7858
www.queenandcompany.com

QuicKutz, Inc.
(888) 702-1146
www.quickutz.com

Ranger Industries, Inc.*
(800) 244-2211
www.rangerink.com

Rhonna Designs
www.rhonnadesigns.com

Rusty Pickle*
(801) 746-1045
www.rustypickle.com

Sakura Hobby Craft
(310) 212-7878
www.sakuracraft.com

Sandylion Sticker Designs
(800) 387-4215
www.sandylion.com

Sassafras Lass
(801) 269-1331
www.sassafraslass.com

Scarlet Lime
www.scarletlime.com

Scenic Route Paper Co.*
(801) 542-8071
www.scenicroutepaper.com

Scrapworks, LLC/
As You Wish Products, LLC
(801) 363-1010
www.scrapworks.com

SEI, Inc.
(800) 333-3279
www.shopsei.com

Shabby Princess
www.shabbyprincess.com

Target
www.target.com

Tattered Tags
www.tatteredtags.etsy.com

Tinkering Ink*
(877) 727-2784
www.tinkeringink.com

Two Peas in a Bucket
(888) 896-7327
www.twopeasinabucket.com

Westrim Crafts
(800) 727-2727
www.westrimcrafts.com

Wrights Ribbon Accents
(877) 597-4448
www.wrights.com

Index

A
Adhesive dots 30, 45
Adhesive storage 15
Albums 13

B
Basic supplies 10-13
BasicGrey 17, 77
blogs 93
Border stickers 56
Brads 49, 88
    organizing 15
Buttons 30, 82
    organizing 15

C
Cardboard 76
Cards 75
Cardstock 10
Catalogs 77, 111
Children's books 110
Chipboard 12, 20
    die-cuts 62
    negative side 78-79
    organizing 16
    undressed 27
Corner rounder 54
Craft supplies 71, 76, 82
Cricut 40
Cropper Hopper 14, 17
Cutting tools 12

D-F
Die-cuts 38, 40, 62
Die-cutting machine 40
Digital
    embellishments 91-92, 95, 101
    layouts 90, 92, 95, 99-101, 103
    templates 64-65, 102-103
Embellishments 12, 23, 65
    organizing 15-16
Fonts 53, 90
Found objects 76
Frames, photo 44-45
    digital 88, 91, 96

G-I
Getting started 8-17
Handwriting 11, 24, 38
Hand-drawing 11, 32
Hidden journaling 35, 75
Image-editing software 89-90, 97, 99, 101
Ink 27, 37, 67, 112
Inspiration 104-119
Inspiration notebook 106

J-M
Journaling 24-25, 35, 38, 50, 53, 61, 75, 89-90
Kit club 47
Magazines 27, 65, 111, 116
Mini albums 85, 102
Monochromatic color scheme 48
Monthly layouts 55, 103

N-P

Neutral background 57
Office supplies 49
Organizing supplies 14-17
Page kits 32, 60
Paper storage 14
Paper tearing 22, 67
Paper trimmers 12
Patterned paper 11, 113
Photos
    arranging digitally 88, 96-97
    enlarging 98
    resizing 88
    standard size, using 69
Photo storage 17, 94
Photoshop 65, 93, 101
Poppy Ink 47
Punches 12, 36
    organizing 16

Q-R

QuicKutz 40
Quotations 34, 106, 115
Ribbon
    frames, using as 45
    organizing 15
    scraps 74, 79
Rub-ons 41, 79
    organizing 16

S

Scraplifting 80, 109
Scraps 72-73, 79, 117
    organizing 73
Sketches 28, 55, 64-65, 80, 97, 101
Stamping 83, 112
Stationery 75
Stickers 49
Stitching 74, 83
    digital 92
    rub-on 41

T-W

Technology, using 86-103
Templates 65, 102-103
Themed product 58-59
Thesaurus 114
Titles 54, 66, 114
Tools, organizing 15
Transparencies 31
Works-in-progress, storing 17
Writing tools, organizing 11

For more ideas for the busy scrapper, check out these other Memory Makers Books.

See what's coming up from Memory Makers Books by checking out our blog:

www.mycraftivity.com/ scrapbooking_ papercrafts/blog/

Ask the Masters:
Organizing Your Scrapbook Supplies

Whether you have a designated scrap room or a coveted seat at the kitchen table, tips from the Memory Makers Masters will get you organized and make you more efficient, more productive and even more creative.

ISBN-13: 978-1-59963-030-4
ISBN-10: 1-59963-030-3

paperback
128 pages
Z2229

Get It Scrapped!

Author and artist Debbie Hodge offers her unique methodology for creating several common page types in this must-have resource for getting layouts scrapped.

ISBN-13: 978-1-59963-015-1
ISBN-10: 1-59963-015-X

paperback
128 pages
Z1597

Scrap Simple

Scrapbooking doesn't have to be fussy to be fun! *Scrap Simple* makes it easy to whip up clean and uncluttered scrapbook pages in a flash.

ISBN-13: 978-1-59963-014-4
ISBN-10: 1-59963-014-1

paperback
128 pages
Z1282

These books and other Memory Makers title are available at your local scrapbook retailer, bookstore or from online suppliers, or visit our Web site at
www.memorymakersmagazine.com
or *www.mycraftivity.com*